KNITTED MINIATURE ANIMALS

KNITTED MINIATURE ANIMALS

Jenny Occleshaw

NEW
HOLLAND

First published in 2014 by
New Holland Publishers
London • Sydney • Cape Town • Auckland
www.newhollandpublishers.com • www.newholland.com.au

The Chandlery Unit 114 50 Westminster Bridge Road London SE1 7QY
1/66 Gibbes Street Chatswood NSW 2067 Australia
Wembley Square First Floor Solan Road Gardens Cape Town 8001 South Africa
218 Lake Road Northcote Auckland New Zealand

A catalogue record of this book is available at the British Library and at the National Library of Australia

ISBN: 9781742575056

10 9 8 7 6 5 4 3 2 1

Publisher: Diane Ward
Project editor: Simona Hill
Designer: Tracy Loughlin
Photographer: Sue Stubbs
Production director: Olga Dementiev
Printer: Toppan Leefung Printing Limited

Follow New Holland Publishers on
Facebook: www.facebook.com/NewHollandPublishers

Contact me at Dropstitchdesign.com with pattern queries.

Contents

Introduction

Welcome to my book of tiny toy knits. This fun collection of domestic, farm and wild animals each have their own personalities, from the party-loving turtle dressed in her best beaded shell, to the magician's rabbit complete with top hat, and the sweet little bluebird of happiness with his angelic face, to the loud and stripy dragon who is looking for a new playmate. Here is something to delight every young child, stretch their make-believe play skills and become a cherished friend. Some of my toys are accessorised with items that add to their personality, Brunhilde the cow, with her decorative sun hat, for instance, or the ballerina penguin, complete with tutu. Once

you've knitted a few items, you'll be able to tailor the accessories and the project to suit the recipient, making your own little animal unique. If you like, you could buy accessories from toy shops. Just make sure that the size is appropriate for the scale of the toy you are making.

I have designed every item in this fabulous new collection to appeal to your sense of fun. These are whimsical creatures that should put a smile on your face and tempt you to dust off your knitting needles and raid your stash of left-over yarn. Since these items are so small, most use minimal yarn quantities, so these projects are great for using up oddments that every keen knitter usually hoards. Being small, they're also relatively quick to make, though almost all are knitted on very fine needles and use yarns more usually associated with baby clothing. Current trends in knitting decorative socks have made small needles and a fabulous assortment of fine yarns widely available.

Every project requires standard knit and purl stitches with the increases and decreases creating the body shaping. Because the body parts knitted are small, they can be a little fiddly. I would really encourage you to take your time when knitting to ensure that you have a firm and even texture so that when the items are stuffed, the filling won't migrate through the fabric. If you're knitting one of the families included here then knit the large one first because it will be easiest to shape. Press each completed item under a fine damp cotton cloth to stop the edges rolling if it helps, and sew the pieces together using tiny stitches. Sometimes the pieces are so small that you'll have to sew them up with the right side out. For this reason it is often best to sew in daylight while sitting at a table.

Fill the toys really firmly with toy stuffing, teasing it out before packing it into the shape. Make sure the stuffing is even too so that your animal isn't mis-shapen. Once the elements are filled and the gaps in the seams that have been used for stuffing are closed, use pins to hold the limbs in place on the main body piece, positioning them all and making sure that you're happy with the arrangement before sewing them in place.

If you choose to add accessories including beads, and you are making an animal for a very young child, ensure that every piece is stitched very firmly in place so that it doesn't loosen and become a hazard.

ABBREVIATIONS

Beg: Beginning.

Cm: Centimetres.

Cont: Continue.

Garter st: Every row knit.

In: Inch.

Inc: Increase by knitting into the front and back of the next stitch.

K: Knit.

Moss st: K1, P1 to end of row. On next row ensure that a purl st sits above a knit st.

M1: Make 1 stitch by picking up the loop that lies between the two needles and knitting into the back of it, then placing it on the right-hand needle.

P: Purl.

PSSO: Pass slipped stitch over.

Rep: Repeat.

Sl: Slip.

St: Stitch or stitches.

St st: Stocking stitch, knit 1 row, purl 1 row.

Rem: Remaining.

RS: Right side.

Tbl: Through back of loops.

Tog: Together.

WS: Wrong side.

Yfwd: Yarn forward.

Yrn: Yarn round needle.

CROCHET ABBREVIATIONS

Ch: Chain.

Dc: Double Crochet.

SS: Slip Stitch.

Tr: Treble Crochet.

DTr: Double Treble.

Tr Tr: Triple Treble.

MAKING AN I-CORD

Using two 2 mm double-pointed knitting needles, cast on 3 sts.

*Knit one row, do not turn, Slide sts to other end of the needle, pull yarn firmly behind the work, rep from * until cord is desired length.

Next row: Sl1, K2tog, psso. Fasten off.

FELTING FABRIC

For a front-loading washing machine: Put the piece to be felted in an empty zipped cushion cover. Load into the machine with a towel and six tennis balls. Set the washing machine to the lowest water level possible and the shortest cycle and wash twice to get the 40 per cent shrinkage.

For a top-loading washing machine, use a short hot cycle with no spin, then quickly immerse the fabric in cold water to cause the felting.

Leave to dry flat. You may need to press the fabric before cutting out the shapes.

Beatrice the Beaded Turtle

This little turtle is all set for a night on the tiles. She has a little beaded bow adorning her head, a spiral of seed beads on her back and a little crocheted ruffle peeking out from under her shell. Beatrice will surely be the belle of the turtle ball. Please note, with so many beads this is not a toy for small children.

MATERIALS

Small amounts (less than 25 g/1 oz) of 4 ply (fingering/ sports weight)) yarn in mid purple, for the shell; bright purple, for the under-shell, head, legs and tail; pink, for the crochet ruffle

Set of 2.25 mm (UK 13/US 1) double-pointed knitting needles

Pair of 2 mm (UK 14/US 0) knitting needles

Wool needle, for sewing up

Polyester toy filling

Black stranded embroidery cotton

Embroidery needle

3 mm (UK 11) crochet hook

Pale purple glass seed beads

Pink glass beads, for the bow

Beading needle

Pink beading thread

Chalk pencil

Shell

The shell is knitted in one piece and in the round. Begin with the upper edge and finish with the underside.

Using 4 x 2.25 mm double-pointed knitting needles and mid purple, cast on 8 sts, (3, 2, 3). Join into a ring, being careful not to twist the sts.

Round 1: Knit.

Round 2: Inc into each st (16 sts).

Round 3: Knit.

Round 4: *Inc, K1, rep from * to end of round (24 sts).

Round 5 and all odd rounds: Knit.

Round 6: *Inc, K2, rep from * to end of round (32 sts).

Round 8: *Inc, K3, rep from * to end of round (40 sts).

Round 10: *Inc, K4, rep from * to end of round (48 sts).

Round 12: *Inc, K5, rep from * to end of round (56 sts).

Round 14: *Inc, K6, rep from * to end of round (64 sts).

Round 16: *Inc, K7, rep from * to end of round (72 sts).

Work another 3 rounds st st without shaping.

Next round: *Yfwd, K2tog, rep from * to end of round.

Knit two rounds.

Change to bright purple for under shell.

Purl 1 round.

Dec round: *K2tog, K7, rep from * to end.

Round 2 and all even rounds: Knit.

Round 3: *K2tog, K6, rep from * to end (56 sts).

Round 5: *K2tog, K5, rep from * to end (48 sts).

Round 7: *K2tog, K4, rep from * to end (40 sts).

Round 9: *K2tog, K3, rep from * to end (32 sts).

Round 11: *K2tog, K2, rep from * to end (24 sts).

Stuff the shell now. When stuffing aim for a flat shape.

Round 13: *K2tog, K1, rep from * to end (16 sts).

Round 15: K2tog 8 times.

Break off yarn, thread through rem sts, pull up tightly and fasten off.

Ruffle

The ruffle is crocheted onto the purl row made just before the colour change for the under-shell.

Using the crochet hook and pink yarn, insert the hook into one of the purl loops. *Ss, 3 ch, ss into the first of the 3 ch. Dc into the next purl loop. Rep from * right around the shell.

Feet

Make 4

Using 2 mm knitting needles and bright purple, cast on 15 sts.

Beg with a knit row, work 5 rows st st.

Next row: P1, P2tog all across.

Break off yarn, thread through rem sts, pull up tightly and fasten off.

Place WS together and sew the side seam. Stuff the legs firmly leaving the tops open. Pin evenly in position on the underside of the turtle. When you are happy with the arrangement, stitch in place using very small stitches.

Tail

Using 2 mm knitting needles and bright purple, cast on 5 sts.

Row 1: Knit.

Row 2: Inc in first st, purl to last st, inc in last st.

Row 3: Knit.

Rep these 2 rows twice more (11 sts).

Work another 2 rows st st.

Next row: P1, (P2tog) 5 times.

Break off yarn, thread through rem sts, pull up tightly and fasten off.

With WS together, sew the side seam. The gathered end will be attached to the turtle. Position under the ruffle and stitch firmly in place.

Head

Using 4 x 2.25 mm double-pointed knitting needles and bright purple, cast on 18 sts, (6, 6, 6). Join into a ring, being careful not to twist the sts.

Round 1: Knit.

Rep this round another 3 times.

Next round: Inc in next st, K5, M1, K12 (20 sts).

Work another 3 rounds st st.

Next round: Sl1, K1, psso, K4, K2tog, K4, K2tog, K6 (17 sts).

Next round: Knit.

Next round: Sl1, K1, psso, K2, K2tog, K5, K2tog, K4 (14 sts).

Next round: Knit.

Next round: Sl1, K1, psso, K1, K2tog, K3, K2tog, K5 (11 sts).

Next round: Knit.

Next round: K6, K2tog, K3 (10 sts).

Next round: K2tog 5 times.

Break off yarn, thread through rem sts, pull up tightly and fasten off.

To make up, fold RS together, stitch the seam and then fill the head with polyester toy filling.

Position on the turtle and sew in place closing the opening as you attach the head to the turtle.

Face

Use a chalk pencil to mark the position of the eyes. Using three strands of black embroidery cotton and an embroidery needle, make a French knot for each eye. Make a large smiley mouth using stem stitch.

Bow

Using 2 mm knitting needles and pink, cast on 8 sts. Work in garter st for 10 rows. Cast off.

Wrap a length of yarn tightly around the centre of the piece to form into a bow. Stitch into place. Using a beading needle and pink beading thread, stitch pink seed beads randomly to the bow. Sew to the top of the turtle's head.

Seed Bead Spiral

Mark a spiral on the upper shell using a chalk pencil. Work from the centre out. The spiral starts close together and becomes wider apart, ending 1 cm (3/8 in) between rows. Sew the beads on one at a time to the drawn line, stitching them really close together. Finish off firmly to stop any beads from coming loose.

Beehive and Bumble Bees

This beehive is a great project for a beginner to felting. It is not very difficult and produces a great looking result. Many different yarns can be felted. I prefer the brand Wash n Filz It! as it is specifically designed for felting. Use the beehive as a pin cushion, if you like.

MATERIALS

2 x 50 g (1¾ oz) balls of Wash n Filz It! fine felting yarn, yellow

Pair of 5 mm (UK 6/US 8) knitting needles

Small amounts (less than 25 g/1 oz) 4-ply (fingering/ sports weight) yarn for the bees in, black, yellow, white

Small amounts (less than 25 g/1 oz) 4-ply (fingering/ sports weight) yarn for the flowers in bright blue, navy blue, bright green

Craft glue

3 mm (UK 11) crochet hook

Set of 4 x 2.25 mm (UK 13/US 1) double-pointed knitting needles

2 mm (UK 14/US 0) double-pointed knitting needles

5 cm (2 in) square of black felt

Dark brown glass seed beads

Beading needle

Beading thread

Polyester toy filling

Wool needle, for sewing up

Sewing needle

Black stranded embroidery cotton

White stranded embroidery cotton

10 cm (4 in) diameter circle of cardboard (card stock)

Yellow polyester thread

Knitting and Felting the Yarn

Using 5 mm knitting needles and yellow felting yarn, cast on 50 sts. Continue in st st until both balls of yarn are used up. Cast off.

For a front-loading washing machine: Put the piece to be felted in an empty zipped cushion cover. Load into the machine with a towel and six tennis balls. Set the washing machine to the lowest water level possible and the shortest cycle and wash twice to get the 40 per cent shrinkage.

For a top-loading washing machine, use a short hot cycle with no spin, then quickly immerse the fabric in cold water to cause the felting.

Leave to dry flat. You may need to press the fabric before cutting out the shapes for the beehive.

Beehive

From the felted fabric cut:

1 circle, 11 cm (4¼ in) diameter, for the base of the beehive.

1 circle 5 cm (2 in) diameter, for the top of the beehive.

1 piece 30 x 5 cm (12 x 2 in), for the bottom ring.

1 piece 23 x 4 cm (9 x 1¾ in), for the second ring.

1 piece 15 x 4 cm (6 x 1¾ in), for the third ring.

1 Glue the cardboard circle in place on the inside of the 11 cm (4¼ in) felted base using craft glue.

2 Roll each of the fabric rectangles for the rings along the long edge and stitch in place to form a sausage using small closely worked stitches. Place the two ends together and stitch closed to make a ring. Place the largest ring on the upper side of the base with the seam facing in and stitch the seamed side of the ring to the base.

3 Stitch each of the smaller rings in place on top of the large ring.

4 Stuff the beehive firmly with polyester toy filling. Put on the top and stitch in place all round, using very small, neat stitches.

5 To make the door, draw a 2.5 cm (1 in) circle on the black felt. Thread the beading needle with beading thread. Cover the circle with the glass seed beads. It is easier to bead the circle before you cut it out. Once the beading is complete, cut out the circle leaving a small margin for stitching all the way around. Place 5 mm (¼ in) above the lover edge of the first layer of the beehive and stitch in position using matching thread.

Flowers

Make 1 bright blue, 1 navy blue, 1 bright green.

Using the crochet hook and bright blue yarn make a slip knot. Make 4 chain, join into a ring.

Round 1: 1 ch, work 8dc into a ring. Ss into first ch.

Round 2: *3 ch, miss 1dc, ss into next dc, rep from * right around the ring ending with ss into first of the 3 ch. Fasten off.

Darn in all ends. Overlap the flowers slightly and stitch to the side of the beehive.

Bees

Make 2

Using set of 4 double-pointed knitting needles and black, cast on 6 sts (2, 2, 2). Join into a ring, being careful not to twist the sts.

Round 1: Knit.

Round 2: Inc in every st (12 sts).

Round 3: Knit.

Round 4: Inc in every st (24 sts).

Round 5: Knit.

Round 6: On each needle K8, K2tog.

Round 7: Knit.

Round 8: K2, K2tog, K5, K2tog, K5, K2tog, K3.

Round 9: Knit.

Round 10: *K1, K2tog, rep from * to end.

Round 11: Knit.

Join in yellow.

Round 12: Inc in every st (24 sts).

Round 13: Knit.

Round 14: K1, inc in next st, K8, inc in next st, K2, inc in next st, K8, inc in next st, K1.

Round 15: Knit.

Change to black. Work 3 rounds st st without further shaping. Change to yellow.

Round 19: Knit

Round 20: Knit.

Round 21: K1, K2tog, K8, K2tog, K2, K2tog, K8, K2tog, K1.

Round 22: Knit.

Change to black.

Round 23: *K2, K2tog, rep from * to end.

Round 24: Knit.

Round 25: *K1, K2tog, rep from * to end.

Fill the bee very firmly with polyester toy filling, making a fat round shape.

Round 26: K2tog (6 times).

Round 27: K2tog (3 times), break off yarn, thread through rem sts, pull up tightly and fasten off.

Wings

Make 2

Using 2 mm knitting needles and white, cast on 3 sts.

Row 1: Knit.

Row 2: Work in garter st throughout. Inc at each end of row (5 sts).

Row 3: Inc at each end of row (7 sts).

Row 4: Knit.

Row 5: Inc at each end of row.

Work 3 rows without further shaping.

Row 9: Sl1, K1, psso, knit to last 2 sts, K2tog.

Row 10: Knit.

Row 11: Sl1, K1, psso, knit to last 2 sts, K2tog.

Row 12: Sl1, K1, psso, knit to last 2 sts, K2tog.

Cast off.

Stitch the bee's wings to the centre of the back noting that the cast-off row is the base of the wing.

Make the antennae by drawing a length of black yarn through the top of the head and knotting it off securely. Take a small stitch of white yarn through the side of the head to form the eyes. Sew one bee to the top of the beehive and the other to the side.

Black-faced Sheep

One of the hardiest breeds of sheep, the black-faced variety is a common sight in the wilds of the countryside. Make this cute little creature or a whole flock of them for the little people in your life. You could try altering the yarn so that your sheep have different colours and coat textures.

MATERIALS

Small amount of cream bouclé fine yarn, equivalent to 4-ply (fingering/sports weight) yarn
Small amount of dark grey 4-ply (fingering/sports weight) yarn, for head and legs
Small amount of orange 4-ply (fingering/sports weight) yarn, for scarf
White stranded embroidery cotton, for eyes and nostrils
Wool needle, for sewing up
Sewing needle
Pair of 2 mm (UK 14/US 0) knitting needles
Pair of 2.25 mm (UK 13/US 1) knitting needles
Polyester toy filling

MEASUREMENTS

Tall: 5 cm (2 in)
Long: 9 cm (3½ in)

Body

Using 2 mm knitting needles and cream bouclé yarn, cast on 7 sts.

Row 1: *K1, yfwd, rep from * to end (13 sts).

Row 2: Purl.

Row 3: K1, *yfwd , K2 rep from * to end (19 sts).

Row 4: Purl

Rep rows 3 and 4 once more (28 sts), ending with K1 (29 sts).

Row 7: Knit.

Row 8: Purl.

Work another 16 rows st st.

Next row: K3, *K2tog, K2, rep from * to last st, K1.

Next row: Purl.

Next row: K2, *K2tog, K1, rep from * to last 2 sts, K2.

Next row: Purl.

Next row: K1, *K2tog all across.

Break off yarn, thread through rem sts, pull up tightly and fasten off.

To make up, fold in half with PURL sides together, stitch two-thirds of the seam closed. Turn right side out. Stuff very firmly with polyester toy filling. Stitch the remainder of the seam closed. Darn in any loose ends.

Head

The face will be dark grey and the top of the head cream.

Using 2 mm knitting needles and cream bouclé, cast on 12 sts.

Row 1: Knit.

Row 2: Purl.

Row 3: Knit.

Break off cream bouclé and join in dark grey.

Work another 4 rows st st beg with a knit row.

Row 8: *Inc, K1, rep from * to end (18 sts).

Work another 7 rows st st, beg with a purl row.

Row 16: (K3, K2tog, Sl1, K1, psso) twice, K2 (14 sts).
Row 17: Purl.
Row 18: (K2, K2tog, Sl1, K1, psso) twice, K2 (10 sts).
Row 19: Purl.
Cast off.
Stitch the centre back seam of the head. Using small pieces of polyester toy filling, stuff the head. Stitch across the top of the cream bouclé section and run a gathering thread around the lower cast-off section of the nose to draw it in. Stitch across at the bottom so it sits fairly flat.
Using cream yarn, stitch the head to the body at the back of the head seam and ensure that it is firmly attached.

Face

Using three strands of white embroidery cotton, make a French knot for each eye 5 mm (¼ in) down from the white section at the top of the head and 7.5 mm (generous ¼ in) in from the side of the head. Work a French knot for each nostril on the underside of the nose, stitching them quite close together.

Ears

Using 2 mm knitting needles and dark grey, cast on 5 sts.
Row 1: K2tog, knit to end.
Row 2: Knit to last 2 sts, K2tog.
Cast off.
Darn in the loose ends, pin to the head just below the cream bouclé section. Stitch in place.

Legs

Make 4
Using 2 mm knitting needles and dark grey, cast on 7 sts. Work 5 rows st st, beg with a knit row.
Break off yarn, thread through rem sts, pull up tightly and fasten off.
Roll up the leg very tightly and stitch down the long seam. Stitch the end closed. Pin to the underside of the body, ensuring that it will be able to stand.

Scarf

Using 2.25 mm knitting needles and orange, cast on 35 sts. Work 2 rows garter st. Cast off. Darn in the ends. Knot around the neck.

Brunhilde the Cow

This cheerful roly poly cow reminds me of those I saw on my childhood holidays staying at a dairy farm. The farmer named the individuals in his herd after opera singers. They were so lovely, trundling up to be milked each morning and night. Brunhilde has a hat to keep off the sun.

MATERIALS

1 x 25 g (1¾ oz) ball of cream 4-ply (fingering/sports weight) yarn
Small amounts of 4-ply (fingering/sports weight) yarn in pale pink, bright pink, black, green and pale blue for the flowers; bright blue, for the hat
Black stranded embroidery cotton
Sewing needle
Polyester toy filling
Set of 4 x 2 mm (UK 14/US 0) knitting needles
Pair of 2.25 mm (UK 13/US 1) knitting needles
Wool needle, for sewing up

Body

Using 4 x 2 mm double-pointed knitting needles and cream, cast on 9 sts (3, 3, 3). Join into a ring, being careful not to twist the sts.

Round 1: Knit.

Round 2: Inc in every st (18 sts).

Rounds 3 and 4: Knit.

Round 5: Inc in every st (36 sts).

Knit another 3 rounds.

Round 9: *K2, inc in next st, rep from * to end of round (48 sts).

Knit 3 rounds.

Round 13: *K2, inc in next st, rep from * to end of round (64 sts).

Knit 2 rounds

Round 16: Inc 3 sts evenly across needle 1, 2 sts across needle 2, and 3 sts across needle 3 (72 sts).

Work another 2.5 cm (1 in) st st without shaping.

Begin decreases:

Round 1: *K2, K2tog rep from * to end of round (54 sts).

Knit 2 rounds.

Round 4: *Sl1, K1, psso, K4, K2tog, rep from * to end of round (36 sts).

Work another 2 cm (¾ in) without further shaping.

Next round: *K4, K2tog, rep from * to end of round.

Stuff the body very firmly, ensuring an even rounded pear shape.

Next round: Knit.

Next round: *K2, K2tog, rep from * to end of round.

Next round: Knit.

Add more stuffing if needed.

Next round: *K1, K2tog, rep from * to end of round.

Next round: *K2 tog, rep all round.

Check stuffing is very firm.

Break off yarn, thread through rem sts, pull up tightly and fasten off.

Head

Begin at nose.

Using 2 mm knitting needles and pink, cast on 18 sts.

Work 2 rows st st.

Next row: K4, (inc 1 st) twice, K5, (inc 1 st) twice, K5.

Purl 1 row.

Next row: K5, (inc 1, K1) twice, K5, (inc1, K1) twice, K5.

St st another 3 rows pink.

Work 1 more row pink increasing 1 st at each end of the row (28 sts).

Change to cream work 7 rows st st beg with a purl row.

Next row: K5, (K2tog, Sl1, K1, psso, K5) twice, end last rep with (K4, K2tog, Sl1, K1, psso, K4) twice. Work 9 rows st st.

Next row: K2tog all across.

Purl 1 row.

Break off yarn, thread through rem sts, pull up tightly and fasten off.

Join the head seam from the gathered top edge down to the base. Stuff the head firmly with polyester toy filling and stitch across the flat underside of the nose. Embroider French knots for nostrils and two French knots with three strands of black embroidery cotton for eyes. Swiss darn the black patches.

Ears

Make 2

Using 2 mm knitting needles and black, cast on 7 sts.

Knit 2 rows.

Next row: Cast on 1 st at beg of row, knit to end.

Next row: Knit, inc in last st.

Cast off.

Darn in the thread ends. Attach the ears to the side of the cow's head with the pointed ends facing outward.

Legs

Make 4

The legs are made using a combination of black and cream yarns. Cast on 4 sts in cream. Work in st st until 2 cm (¾ in) have been worked, break off colour and join in black.

To finish Sl2, K2tog, psso. Fasten off. Work 2 legs this way and 2 legs beg in black and ending in cream.

Hooves

Make 4

Using 2 x 2 mm knitting needles and black, cast on 1 st. K, P, K, P, K, P into the front and back of the same st (6 sts).

Row 1: Knit.

Row 2: Purl.

Row 3: Knit.

Row 4: Purl.

Row 5: K1, *Slip second st on needle over first, rep from * until 1 st rem. Fasten off. Run a gathering thread around the bobble, draw up to form a neat round shape. Sew onto the end of each leg. Sew the legs on to the front of the cow. Place the back legs wider than the front.

Tail

Make a 5 cm (2 in), 3-st I-cord from cream. Add a little fringe to one end using short lengths of black. Fasten securely. Attach the tail to the cow's bottom.

Hat

Brim

Using blue yarn and 2.25 mm needles, cast on 60 sts.

Work 6 rows garter st.

Row 7: *K1, K2tog, rep from * to end (36 sts).

Work another 3 rows garter st.

Cast off. Stitch row ends together.

Hat Top

Using blue, cast on 36 sts.

Work 14 rows st st.

Next row: *K1, K2tog, rep from * to end.

Next row: Purl.

Next row: K2tog all across.

Break off yarn, thread through rem sts, pull up tightly and fasten off.

With RS facing, stitch row ends tog and turn RS out. Stitch the cast-off edge of hat brim to the cast-on edge of hat top.

Flowers

Make 2 pink, 1 green, 1 blue

Using 2 mm knitting needles and colour of your choice, cast on 16 sts.

Row 1: Purl.

Row 2: K2tog all across.

Break off yarn. Sew row ends together and form into a neat circle. Sew on the flowers.

Sew the hat to the top of the head, if desired, or leave it so that it can be taken on and off.

Little Grey Mouse

This adorable little mouse with his large pink ears and shiny black bead eyes is looking for a playmate. With his cord-like arms and legs he is quick to knit and is sure to inspire hours of make-believe fun play.

MATERIALS

Small amount (less than 25 g/1 oz) grey 4-ply (fingering/sports weight) yarn

Small amount pink 4-ply (fingering/sports weight) yarn, for inner ear

Set of 2.25 mm (UK 13/US 1) double-pointed knitting needles

Polyester toy filling

Wool needle, for sewing up

Black stranded embroidery cotton, for the whiskers

Sewing needle

2 small black beads, for the eyes

Head

Using grey, cast on 9 sts (3, 3, 3). Join into a ring.
Round 1: Knit.
Round 2: K1, M1 in next st, K1, on each needle (15 sts).
Round 3: Knit.
Round 4: K1, M1 in next st, K1, M1 in next st, K1 (21 sts).
Knit 4 rounds.
Round 9: K1, K2tog, K1, K2tog, K1 (15 sts).
Knit 2 rounds.
Round 12: Sl1, K1, psso, K1, K2tog (9 sts).
Round 13: Knit.
Leaving sts on needle, stuff head firmly. Run thread through rem sts, pull up tightly and fasten off. Set aside for later.

Body

Using grey, cast on 9 sts (3, 3, 3). Join into a ring.
Round 1: Knit.
Round 2: K1, M1 in next st, K1, on each needle (15 sts).
Round 3: Knit.
Round 4: K1, M1 in next st, K1, M1 in next st, K1 (21 sts).
Round 5: Knit.
Round 6: K1, M1 in next st, K3, M1 in next st, K1 (27 sts).
Knit 9 rounds.
Round 16: Sl1, K1, psso, K5, K2tog on each needle (21 sts).
Round 17: Knit.
Round 18: Sl1, K1, psso, K3, K2tog, on each needle (15 sts).
Round 19: Knit.
Round 20: Sl1, K1, psso, K1, K2tog, on each needle (9 sts).
Round 21: Knit.
Leaving sts on needle, stuff body firmly. Run thread through rem sts, pull up tightly and fasten off. Set aside.

Ears

Make 2 in grey
Make 2 linings in pink
Using yarn, and working backwards and forwards in rows, cast on 2 sts.
Row 1 and all odd rows: Purl.
Row 2: K1, M1 in next st.
Row 4: Inc in first and last st.
Work 2 rows without shaping.
Row 7: K2tog, K1, K2tog.
Row 8: Purl.
Cast off.
Using three strands of pink embroidery cotton, satin stitch the inner ear. To attach to the head, pinch the lower edges together and firmly sew to the sides of the mouse's head.

I-cord Legs and Arms

Make two arms 3 cm (1¼ in) long
Make two legs 4 cm (1¾ in) long
To make an I cord, using grey, cast on 3 sts.
Row 1: *Knit.
Do not turn, slide sts to the other end of the needle, pull yarn firmly behind the work and repeat the first row. Continue in this manner until the cord is the desired length. To finish off, Sl1, K2tog psso, fasten off.

Feet and Paws

These are bobbles and are stitched to the end of the legs or the arms. Make 4
Using grey, cast on 1 st.
K, P, K, P, K, into this stitch, making 5 stitches. Turn.
Next row: Purl.
Next row: Knit.
Next row: Purl.
Next row: Knit. Slip the second stitch over the first stitch on the right-hand needle. Cont in this manner until 1 st rem. Break off yarn. Thread through st. Pull up tightly and fasten off. To form into a bobble, run a gathering st around the outside, draw up and fasten off, forming a circular shape. Attach one to each arm and leg.

Assembling the Mouse

Sew the head to the body with the pointy nose facing forward and the widest part of the body as the base. Using three strands of black embroidery cotton, make a French knot for each eye and fasten off invisibly where the head joins the body.
Using pink embroidery cotton, make a French knot for the nose. Sew the arms at shoulder height and the legs at hip height on each side of the body. Make sure you attach all parts very firmly.

Tail

Make a 2-st I-cord 6 cm (2¼ in) long. Attach to mouse firmly.

Custard the Dragon

With his scaly back and feet, this little dragon looks like a fearsome comrade who is ready for battle. In actual fact, he's a scaredy cat who is as meek as a mouse. Though this looks like a complicated pattern, Custard is not too difficult to make and is well worth the effort.

MATERIALS

Small amount (less than 25 g/1 oz) Noro Kureyon Sock Yarn 4-ply (or other 4-ply (fingering/sports weight) yarn)

2 x 6 mm (¼ in) black beads, for the eyes

Set of 2.25 mm (UK 13/US 1) double-pointed knitting needles

Polyester toy filling

Wool needle, for sewing up

Long doll-making needle

Black stranded embroidery cotton

Sewing needle

Note

Making the dragon is similar to knitting a sock. He is mostly knitted in the round, though there are some turnings to give his tummy shaping. When you make the turns slip the next st onto the right-hand needle bring the yarn to the front and then slip the sts back on to the left-hand needle. This prevents holes in the knitting and is described in the instructions as (wp)

Head

Using 4 x 2.25 mm double-pointed knitting needles and Noro Kureyon yarn, cast on 9 sts (3, 3, 3). Join into a ring, being careful not to twist the stitches.

Round 1: Knit.
Round 2: *K1, inc, K1, rep from * to end.
Round 3: *K1, inc, K2, rep from * to end (15 sts).
Round 4: *K2, inc, K2, rep from * to end (18 sts).
Round 5: *K2, inc, K3, rep from * to end (21 sts).
Round 6: *K3, inc, K3, rep from * to end (24 sts).
Round 7: *K3, inc, K4, rep from * to end (27 sts).
Round 8: *K4, inc, K4, rep from * to end (30 sts).
Round 9: *K4, inc, K5, rep from* to end (33 sts).
Round 10: *K5, inc, K5, rep from *to end (36 sts).
Work another 6 rounds st st without shaping.
Round 17: K8, K2tog, K4, K2togtbl, K20 (34 sts).
Round 18: K7, K2tog, K4, K2togtbl, K19 (32 sts).
Round 19: K6, K2tog, K4, K2togtbl, K18 (30 sts).
Round 20: K5, K2tog, K4, K2togtbl, K7, Ktog, K4, K2togtbl, K2 (26 sts).
Round 21: K4, K2tog, K4, K2togtbl, K5, K2tog, K4, K2togtbl, K1 (22 sts).
Round 22: K3, K2tog, K4, K2togtbl, K11 (20 sts).
Work 10 rounds st st.
Round 33: K2tog all round.
Work 3 rounds st st.
Stuff the head firmly with polyester toy filling.
Round 37: K2tog all round.
Break off yarn, thread through rem sts, pull up tightly and fasten off.

Body

Cast on 15 sts (5, 5, 5). Join into a ring, being careful not to twist the stitches.
Knit 7 rounds st st (every round knit).
Round 8: K7, M1, K8 (16 sts).

Work 2 rounds st st.
Round 11: K8, M1, K8 (17 sts).
Round 12: Knit.
Round 13: M1, K17 (18 sts).
Round 14: K18, M1 (19 sts).
Round 15: K3, M1, K13, M1, K3 (21 sts).
Round 16: M1, knit to end.
Round 17: K3, M1, K8, M1, K9, M1, K2 (25 sts).
Round 18: Knit.
Round 19: K5, (wp) turn P10, (wp) turn, K5, K13, K5 (25 sts).
Round 20: K3, M1, K10, M1, K9, M1, K3 (28 sts).
Round 21: K6 (wp) turn, P12, (wp) turn, K12, K2, M1, K11, M1, K1, K11, K6 (30 sts).
Round 22: K3, M1, K24, M1, K3 (32 sts).
Round 23: K7, (wp), turn, P14, (wp), turn, K7, K16, K7 (32 sts).
Round 24: K3, M1, K26, M1, K3 (34 sts).
Round 25: K8, (wp), turn, P16, (wp), turn, K8, K8, K16, K8 (34 sts).
Round 26: K8, (wp), turn, P16, (wp), turn, K15, (wp), turn, P14, (wp), turn, K13, (wp), turn, P12, (wp), turn, K11, (wp), turn, P10, (wp), turn, K9, (wp), turn, P8, (wp), turn, K4,
Round 27: K4, K5, K16, K5, K4 (34 sts).
Round 28: K2tog, K to end to round (33 sts).
Round 29: K13, K2togtbl, K4, K2tog, K12 (31 sts).
Round 30: K6, (wp), turn, P12 (wp) turn, K17, K1, K2tog, K3 (29 sts).
Round 31: Knit.
Round 32: K3, K2togtbl, K19, K2tog, K3 (27 sts).
Round 33: Knit.
Round 34: K3, K2tog, K8 (26 sts).
Round 35: K8, K2togtbl, K16 (25 sts).
Round 36: K4, (wp) turn, P8, (wp) turn, K8, K15, K2, K2tog (24 sts).

Round 37: Knit.

Round 38: K6, K2togtbl, K16 (23 sts).

Round 39: K15, K2tog, K6 (22 sts).

Round 40: K2tog, K20 (21 sts).

Round 41: Knit.

Round 42: K5, K2togtbl, K14 (20 sts).

Round 43: K12, K2tog, K6 (19 sts).

Round 44: K17, K2tog (18 sts).

Round 45: Knit.

Round 46: K5, K2togtbl, K11 (17 sts).

Round 47: K10, K2tog, K5 (16 sts).

Round 48: K15, K2tog, *the last st of this round will be knitted together with the first st of the next round. This forms part of the decrease.

Round 49: Knit.

Round 50: K4, K2togtbl, K9 (14 sts).

Round 51: K7, K2tog, K5 (13 sts).

Rounds 52–54: Knit.

Round 55: K2, K2togtbl, K8 (11 sts).

Round 56: K5, K2tog, K4 (10 sts).

Round 57: K9, K2tog, *the last st of this round will be knitted tog with the first st of the next round. This forms part of the decrease.

Round 58: Knit.

Round 59: K2, K2togtbl, K5 (8 sts).

Round 60: K3, K2tog, K3 (7 sts).

Round 61: K5, K2tog (6 sts).

Round 62: K2tog, 3 times.

Break off yarn, thread through rem sts, pull up tightly and fasten off. Stuff body very firmly with polyester toy filling. Don't close neck end. Pin head to neck. Stitch head to neck using very small stitches and making sure that you have sufficient stuffing in the neck area so that the head does not wobble.

Back Legs

Make 2

Left Leg

Using 2 x 2.25 mm double-pointed needles held in the right hand and main colour, cast on 10 sts (5 on each needle) Note: This is the method used for toe-up style socks.

Round 1: Knit.

Round 2: (K1, M1, K3, M1, K1) twice (14 sts) *divide knitting on to three needles.

Work 6 rounds st st.

Round 9: K2tog, K10, K2togtbl.

Work 6 rounds st st.

Round 16: K3, M1, K9.

Round 17: K3, M1, K10.

Round 18: K4, M1, K10.

Round 19: K4, M1, K11.

Round 20: K5, M1, K11.

Round 21: K5, M1, K12.

Round 22: Knit.

Round 23: K6, M1, K12.

Work 5 rounds st st.

Round 29: K6, Sl2, K1 psso, K10 (17 sts).

Round 30: Knit.

Round 31: K4, Sl2, K1, psso, K10 (15 sts).

Round 32: K3, Sl2, K1, psso, K5, K2tog, K2 (12 sts).

Stuff the leg firmly.

Round 33: K2, Sl2, K1, psso, K3, K2tog, K2 (9 sts).

Round 34: K1, Sl2, K1, psso, K1, K2tog, K2 (6 sts).

Break off yarn, thread through rem sts, pull up tightly and fasten off

Right Leg

Work as for left leg up to and including round 8.

Round 9: K2togtbl, K10, K2tog.

Work 6 rounds st st.

Round 16: K3, M1, K9.

Round 17: K3, M1, K10.

Round 18: K4, M1, K10.

Round 19: K4, M1, K11.

Round 20: K5, M1, K11.

Round 21: K5, M1, K12.

Round 22: Knit.

Round 23: K6, M1, K12.

Work 5 rounds st st.

Round 29: K6, Sl2, K1 psso, K10 (17 sts).

Round 30: Knit.

Round 31: K4, Sl2, K1, psso, K10 (15 sts).

Round 32: K3, Sl2, K1, psso, K5, K2tog, K2 (12 sts). Stuff the leg firmly.

Round 33: K2, Sl2, K1, psso, K3, K2tog, K2 (9 sts).

Round 34: K1, Sl2, K1, psso, K1, K2tog, K2 (6 sts).

Break off yarn, thread through rem sts, pull up tightly and fasten off

Attach the leg far back on the body using the long doll-making needle sewing right through the body and out the other side. Pull the yarn through firmly so that the legs will sit flat against the body.

Front Legs

Make 2

Using 4 x 2.25 mm double-pointed knitting needles and main colour, cast on 9 sts (3, 3, 3). Join into a ring being careful not to twist the sts.

Round 1: Knit.

Round 2: K1 inc in next st K1, rep twice (14 sts).

Work 5 rounds st st without shaping.

Round 8: K1, K2tog, K3, K2tog, K6 (12 sts).

Work 3 rounds st st.

Round 12: K9 (wp) turn P6, (wp) turn, K6, K2.

Round 13: K2, K9.

Round 14: Knit.

Repeat last 3 rounds twice more.

Round 21: Knit.

Round 22: (K1, K2tog, K1) three times. Stuff the arms firmly.

Round 23: (K1, K2tog) three times.

Break off yarn, thread through rem sts, pull up tightly and fasten off.

Nostrils

Make 2

Using 2 x 2.25 mm double-pointed knitting needles, cast on 1 st. Knit into the front, back and front of the same st (3 sts).

Row 1: Knit.

Row 2: Purl.

Row 3: Knit, do not turn, *slip second st on needle over the first, rep from * until 1 st rems. Fasten off. Run a gathering thread around the outside of the bobble and draw up to form a tiny ball. Attach to each side of the dragon's nose.

Buttons

Make 3

Make as for the nostrils using 4 stitches instead of 3. Attach to the tummy, evenly spaced.

Ears

Make 2

Because the ears are quite small it is easier to knit them on 2 needles and use the third needle for working. They will still be knitted in the round but the knitting will have a more even texture.

Using 3 x 2.25mm double-pointed needles and yarn, cast on 6 sts on two needles (hold the two needles parallel and use the third for knitting).

Round 1: Knit.

Round 2: Knit.

Round 3: M1, K6, M1.

Round 4: K1, M1, K3, M1, K1, M1, K3, M1 (12 sts).

Round 5: K1, M1, K10, M1, K1 (14 sts).

Round 6: Knit.

Round 7: K1, M1, K12, M1, K1 (16 sts).

Round 8: Knit.

Round 9: Knit.

Round 10: Sl1, K1, psso, K12, K2tog.

Round 11: Knit.

Round 12: Sl1, K1, psso, K3, K2tog, Sl1, K1, psso, K3, K2tog.

Round 13: Sl1, K1, psso, K6, K2tog (8 sts).

Round 14: Sl1, K1, psso, K2tog, Sl1, K1, psso, K2tog (4 sts).

Round 15: Knit.

Break off yarn, thread through rem sts, pull up tightly and fasten off. Attach to the head.

Scales

These are knitted as for the ears. Add as many or as few as you like.

Using 3 x 2.25 mm double-pointed knitting needles and yarn, cast on 16 sts on 2 needles (hold the 2 needles parallel and use the third for knitting).

Round 1: Knit.

Round 2: Sl1, K1, psso, K4, K2tog, Sl1, K1, psso, K4, K2tog (12 sts).

Round 3: Knit.

Round 4: Sl1, K1, psso, K2, Sl1, K1, psso, K2, K2tog (8 sts).

Round 5: Knit

Round 6: Sl1, K1, psso, K2tog, Sl1, K1, psso, K2tog.

Round 7: Knit.

Round 8: Sl1, K1, psso, Sl1, K1, psso.

Break off yarn, thread through rem sts, pull tightly and fasten off.

Make sufficient scales to fit along the dragon's tail plus one for the top of the head. Darn in all ends securely and stitch in place.

Make an extra scale for each toe by casting on 8 sts instead of 16 and knitting one row before starting to decrease. Attach securely to each toe.

Dougal the Dog

This little dog has pose-able legs, though being a young puppy he hasn't quite grown into them, or mastered the art of standing still for a long time. Sitting on his lovely soft blanket is more his thing.

MATERIALS

Small amount (less than 25 g/1 oz) of variegated 4-ply (fingering/sports weight) yarn (an oddment of sock yarn is ideal)

Small amount of dark brown 4-ply (fingering/sports weight) yarn, for the tail and ears

Small amount of red 4-ply (fingering/sports weight) yarn, for the collar and blanket

1 pair of 2.25 mm (UK 13/US 1) knitting needles

1 pair of 3.25 mm (UK 10/US 3) knitting needles

1 small blue felt heart

Blue stranded embroidery cotton

Wool needle, for sewing up

Sewing needle

2 x 3 mm (⅛ in) black beads, for the eyes

Polyester toy filling

MEASUREMENTS

10 cm (4 in) long x 7 cm (2¾ in) tall.

Body

Using 2.25 mm knitting needles and variegated yarn, cast on 10 sts.

Row 1: Knit.

Row 2: Purl.

Row 3: *K1, inc in next st, rep from * to end (15 sts).

Row 4: Purl.

Row 5: Inc in every st to end (30 sts).

Beg with a purl row, work another 30 rows st st.

Row 36: K2tog all across (15 sts).

Row 37: Purl.

Row 38: K2tog all across.

Break off yarn, thread through rem sts, pull up tightly and fasten off.

With RS facing stitch together the long seam, (this seam will be underneath the puppy) for two-thirds of the way. Turn RS out. Stuff firmly with polyester toy filling to create a rounded shape. Stitch the rest of the seam closed. Set aside.

Head

Using 2.25 mm knitting needles and variegated yarn, cast on 5 sts.

Row 1: Purl.

Row 2: Inc in every st to end (10 sts).

Row 3: Purl.

Row 4: Inc in every st to end (20 sts).

Row 5: Purl.

Row 6: *Inc in next st, K1, rep from * to end (30 sts).

Work another 22 rows st st, beg with a purl row.

Row 29: *K1, K2tog, rep from * to end (20 sts).

Row 30: Purl.

Row 31: *K1, K2tog, rep from * to last 2 sts, K2.

Row 32: Purl.

Row 33: K2tog all across.

Break off yarn, thread through rem sts, pull up tightly and fasten off.

With RS together, sew centre back head seam two-thirds of the way closed. Turn RS out. Stuff the head firmly with polyester toy filling. Stitch closed the remainder of the seam.

Muzzle

Using 2.25 mm knitting needles and dark brown yarn, cast on 6 sts.

Row 1: Inc in first st, knit, inc in last st.

Row 2: Purl.

Row 3: Inc in first st, knit, inc in last st (10 sts).

Work another 8 rows st st.

Row 12: K2tog, K6, K2tog.

Row 13: Purl.

Row 14: K2tog, K4, K2tog.

Cast off.

Place the muzzle lengthways across the head approximately two-thirds of the way down from the top. Pin in place. Place a little polyester toy filling inside the muzzle and then stitch all around.

Eyes

Sew the two blacks beads in place just above the muzzle and approximately 1 cm (3/8 in) apart. If you are making the project for a small child, embroider the eyes using three strands of black embroidery cotton and French knots instead.

Ears

Make 2

Using 2.25 mm knitting needles and dark brown yarn, cast on 7 sts.

Row 1: Inc in first st, knit, inc in last st (9 sts).

Work another 11 rows garter st.

Row 12: K1, K2tog, K3, K2tog, K1.

Work another 11 rows garter st.

Row 24: K1, K2tog, K1, K2tog, K1.

Row 25: K2tog, K1, K2tog.

Cast off.

Pin the cast-on ends to the top of the head approximately 1 cm (3/8 in) down from the top and evenly spaced at each side of the head. Stitch in place using very small stitches. Darn in any loose ends. Attach the head to the end of the body taking a number of stitches through the cast-on end of the body and head and ensuring that it is firmly attached and does not wobble. The head should sit up about 5 mm (¼ in) higher than the top of the dog's back.

Legs

Make 4

Using 2.25 mm knitting needles and variegated yarn, cast on 9 sts.

Row 1: Purl.

Row 2: Inc in each st (18 sts).

Row 3: Purl.

Row 4: K7, (inc in next st) four times, K7 (22 sts).

Work 3 rows st st.

Row 8: K5, K2tog, K1, K2tog, K2, K2tog, K1, K2tog, K5 (18 sts).

Row 9: Purl.

Row 10: K3, K2tog, K1, K2tog, K2, K2tog, K1, K2tog, K3 (14 sts).

Row 11: Purl.

Work 11 rows st st.

Row 23: K3, K2tog, K4, K2tog, K3 (12 sts).

Row 24: Purl.

Row 25: K3, K2tog, K2, K2tog, K3 (10 sts).

Row 26: Purl.

Row 27: K2tog all across.

Break off yarn, thread through rem sts, pull up tightly and fasten off.

Stitch the back seam, leaving a little gap for stuffing. Fill firmly with polyester toy filling. Close the remainder of the seam. Run a gathering thread around the cast-on stitches and pull up tightly so that there is no gap showing.

Pin the legs to the dog so that they are evenly placed and then stitch in place running the thread through the body to the next leg. The legs should move quite easily so that the puppy will be able to sit or stand.

Collar

Using 2 x 2.25 mm double-pointed knitting needles and red yarn, cast on 3 sts.

Make an I-cord just long enough to fit around the dog's neck (see introduction).

Sl1, K2tog, psso. Fasten off. Fasten around the dog's neck and stitch into place.

Blanket

Using 3.25 mm knitting needles and red, cast on 35 sts. Work in garter st for 58 rows. Cast off.

Using three strands of blue embroidery thread, work blanket st around the outside of the blanket. Sew the blue felt heart on to one corner.

Magician's Rabbit

Now you see him... just wait for the magician's tap of the wand and see if he disappears. Hat and rabbit are quick and eay to knit and will make a delightful gift for any magic-inspired youngster who wants to test his or her sleight of hand.

Materials

Small amount (less than 25 g/1 oz) white 4-ply (fingering/sports weight) cotton for the rabbit

Oddment of pink 4-ply (fingering/sports weight), for the ear linings

Oddment of blue 4-ply (fingering/sports weight), for the scarf

Small amount (less than 25 g/1 oz) black 4-ply (fingering/sports weight), for the hat

Oddment of red 4-ply (fingering/sports weight), for the brim of the hat

Set of 2.25 mm (UK 13/US 1) double-pointed knitting needles

Pair of 2 mm (UK 14/US 0) knitting needles

Wool needle, for sewing up

Sewing needle

Polyester toy filling

Black stranded embroidery cotton, for the eyes

Pink stranded embroidery cotton, for the nose

Cardboard (card stock), to line the top of the hat

Glue

Small piece of black felt (optional)

Head

Using white and 2.25 mm needles, cast on 9 sts (3, 3, 3). Join into a ring.

Round 1: Knit.

Round 2: K1, M1, K1 to end (15 sts).

Round 3: Knit.

Round 4: K1, M1, K3, M1, K1 on each needle (21 sts).

Rounds 5–8: Knit.

Round 9: K1, K2tog, K1, K2tog, K1 on each needle (15 sts).

Rounds 10–11: Knit.

Round 12: Sl1, K1, psso, K1, K2tog on each needle (9 sts).

Round 13: Knit.

Leaving sts on needle, stuff head firmly. Run thread through rem sts, pull up tightly and fasten off. Set aside for later.

Body

Using white and 2.25 mm needles, cast on 9 sts (3, 3, 3). Join into a ring.

Round 1: Knit.

Round 2: K1, M1, K1 to end (15 sts).

Round 3: Knit.

Round 4: K1, M1, K3, M1, K1 on each needle (21 sts).

Round 5: Knit.

Round 6: K1, M1, K5, M1, K1 on each needle (27 sts).

Rounds 7–15: Knit.

Round 16: Sl1, K1, psso, K5, K2tog on each needle (21 sts).

Round 17: Knit.

Round 18: Sl1, K1, psso, K3, K2tog to end (15 sts).

Round 19: Knit.

Round 20: Sl1, K1, psso, K1, K2tog, on each needle (9 sts).

Round 21: Knit.

Leaving sts on needle, stuff body firmly. Run thread through rem sts, pull up tightly and fasten off. Set aside.

Ears

Make 2 from white cotton

Make 2 linings from pink yarn.

Using white cotton and 2 x 2.25 mm needles, and working backward and forward in rows, cast on 2 sts.

Row 1 and all odd rows: Purl.

Row 2: K1, M1, K1.

Row 4: K1, M1, K1, M1, K1.

Work 15 rows st st ending with a purl row.

Row 20: K2tog, K1, K2tog.

Row 21: Purl.

Cast off. Carefully stitch an ear and an ear lining together with WS facing. Turn RS out.

Legs and Arms

Make 2 arms each 3 cm (1¼ in) long

Make 2 legs each 4 cm (1½ in) long

The legs and arms are knitted I-cords. To make an I-cord, using 2 x 2/25 mm double-pointed knitting needles and white cotton, cast on 3 sts.

Row 1: *Knit.

Do not turn, slide sts to the other end of the needle, pull yarn firmly behind the work and repeat row 1. Cont in this manner until the I-cord is the desired length. To finish, Sl1, K2tog, psso. Fasten off.

Feet, Paws and Tail

Make 5

Using 2 x 2.25 mm needles and white cotton, cast on 1 st.

Row 1: K, P, K, P, K into the back and front of the same st (5 sts).

Row 2: Purl.

Row 3: Knit

Row 4: Purl.

Row 5: Knit. Do not turn. Slip the second st over the first st on the right-hand needle. Cont in this manner until 1 st remains. Break off yarn. Thread through st. Pull up tightly and fasten off. To form into a bobble, run a gathering st around the outside, draw up and fasten off, forming into a circular bobble. Attach one to each arm and leg and keep one for the tail.

Assembling the Rabbit

Sew the head to the body with the pointy nose facing forward. Position the ears on each side of the head, holding them in place with pins while you sew them on. Using three strands of pink embroidery cotton, work a few short stitches across and one or two down for the nose. For the eyes, use three strands of black embroidery cotton and work a couple of short stitches on each side of the head, or make French knot eyes. Fasten off in the neck area.

Firmly stitch a leg to each side of the lower body, and an arm to each side of the upper body at the shoulder point.

Scarf

Using 2.25 mm double-pointed knitting needles and blue yarn and working backwards and forwards in rows, cast on 3 sts.

Work in K1, P1 rib for 11 cm (4¼ in). Cast off.

Darn in the ends. Tie in a knot around the rabbit's neck.

Top Hat

Brim

Using 2 mm knitting needles and black, cast on 61 sts.

Row 1: Purl.

Row 2: *K2, inc in next st, rep from * to last st, K1.

Work another 6 rows st st.

Row 9: Knit.

Work another 8 rows st st, beg with a knit row.

Row 18: *K2, K2tog, rep from * to last st, K1.

Row 19: Purl.

Cast off.

Crown

Using 2 mm knitting needles and black, cast on 55 sts.

Beg with a knit row, work 12 rows st st.

Row 13: Purl.

Work another 20 rows st st.

Shape Top

Row 1: *K3, K2tog, rep from * to end.

Row 2: and all even rows: Purl.

Row 3: *K2, K2tog, rep from * to end.

Row 5: *K1, K2tog, rep from * to end.

Row 7: K2tog all across.

Break off yarn, thread through rem sts, pull up tightly and fasten off.

Fold the lining of the crown to the inside.

Hat Band

Using 2.25 mm double-pointed knitting needles and red, cast on 3 sts. Work an I-cord long enough to fit, just around the base of the hat. Fasten off. Position and stitch in place.

With RS together, join the row ends. Fold the piece into a circle, place over the crown and stitch to the lower edge. Cut a piece of cardboard the same diameter as the hat crown and insert in place.

Spike the Echidna

Ant-eater or hedgehog? This sweet little creature is just the right size for a small child to play with and carry in his pocket. Be sure to stitch the bead nose on securely. Why not make a whole family using different yarn textures and shades to give different effects?

MATERIALS

1 x 50 g (1¾ oz) brown fancy eyelash yarn
Small amount (less than 25 g/1 oz) beige 4-ply
   (fingering/sports weight) yarn, for the snout and feet
Pair of 2.25 mm (UK 13/US 1) knitting needles
2 x 2.25 mm (UK 13/US 1) double-pointed knitting
   needles
Black stranded embroidery cotton
Sewing needle
1 x 3 mm (¹/₈ in) black bead
Polyester toy filling
Wool needle, for sewing up

Body

Using 2.25 mm knitting needles and eyelash yarn, cast on 7 sts.

Row 1: *K1, yfwd, rep from * to end (13 sts).

Row 2: Purl.

Row 3: K1, *yfwd, K2, rep from * to end (19 sts).

Row 4: Purl.

Rep last 2 rows once (28 sts).

Work another 18 rows st st.

Row 25: K3, (K2tog, K3, five times), K1 (24 sts).

Break off eyelash yarn and join in beige.

Knit 1 row.

Row 27: Purl.

Row 28: Knit.

Row 29: Purl.

Row 30: K3, (K2tog, K2, five times), K1 (19 sts).

Row 31: Purl.

Row 32: K2, (K2tog, K1, five times), K1 (13 sts).

Row 33: Purl.

Row 34: Knit.

Row 35: Purl.

Row 36: Knit.

Break off yarn, thread through rem sts, pull up tightly and fasten off.

Stitch the underbody seam, leaving a gap for stuffing.

Fill firmly with polyester toy filling, especially the nose.

Close the remainder of the seam.

Legs

Make 4

Using 2 x 2.25 mm double-pointed knitting needles and beige, cast on 1 st. K, P, K, P, K, all into same st (5 sts).

Row 1: Knit.

Row 2: Purl.

Row 3: Knit.

Row 4: Purl.

Row 5: Knit, do not turn, *slip second st on right-hand needle over first, rep from * until 1 st rem. Fasten off. Run a gathering thread around the outside of the bobble and draw up to make a rounded shape. Darn in any loose ends. Pin the legs into place on the underside of the body. Stitch in position.

Face

Stitch the bead in position on the tip of the nose and work French knots for eyes using black embroidery cotton.

Elephant Family

These elephants are all variations of the same pattern. They are knitted in the round with their ears, legs and tails attached once the main part of the knitting is complete. Trunks are fun to make and you can make them as long as you like and curve them up or down so that each can express a different personality.

MATERIALS

Less than 25 g (1 oz) of 4-ply (fingering/sports weight) yarn for each elephant, in your choice of colour

Set of 2.25 mm (UK 13/US 1) double-pointed knitting needles

Wool needle, for sewing up

Polyester toy filling

Black stranded embroidery cotton, for the eyes

Pa Elephant
Body

Using 4-ply yarn, cast on 8 sts (3, 2, 3). Join into a ring, being careful not to twist the sts.

Round 1: Knit.

Round 2: Inc in each st (16 sts).

Rounds 3 and 4: Knit.

Round 5: *K1, inc in next st, rep from * to end of round (24 sts).

Rounds 6 and 7: Knit.

Round 8: *K2, inc in next st, rep from * to end of round (32 sts).

Rounds 9–11: Knit.

Round 12: *K3, inc in next st, rep from * to end of round (40 sts).

Rounds 13 and 14: Knit.

Round 15: *K5, M1, rep from * to end of round (48 sts).

Rounds 16 and 17: Knit.

Round 18: *K6, M1, rep from * to end of round (56 sts).

Work another 30 rounds without shaping.

Dec round: *K4, Sl1, K1, psso, rep from * to last 2 sts, K2 (47 sts).

Knit 3 rounds.

Next round: *K3, Sl1, K1, psso, rep from * to last 2 sts, K2 (38 sts).

Knit 2 rounds.

Next round: *K4, Sl1, K1, psso, rep from * to last 2 sts, K2 (32 sts).

Knit 2 rounds.

Next round: *K3, Sl1, K1, psso, rep from * to last 2 sts K2 (26 sts).

Knit 1 round.

Next round: *K2, Sl1, K1, psso rep from * to last 2 sts, K2 (20 sts)

knit another 28 rounds for the trunk.

Picot round: K1, *yfwd, K2tog, rep from * to last st, K1.

Knit another 5 rounds.

At this point stuff the elephant firmly through the trunk. The knitting will still be on the needles, but if you proceed any further you won't be able to stuff the toy. Do not over-fill the trunk as you want it to be bendy. *K2tog, rep from * to end of round (10 sts).

Next round: *K2tog, rep from * to end of round. Break off yarn, thread through rem sts, pull up tightly and push the end of the trunk back inside itself, so that it is folded at the picot edge.

Legs

Make 4

Cast on 16 sts.

Work 8 rows st st.

Next row: K2tog all across.

Break off yarn, thread through rem sts, pull up tightly and fasten off.

With RS facing, sew row ends together. Turn RS out. Stuff firmly with polyester toy filling. Pin to underside of elephant and stitch in position all around.

Ears

Make 2

Cast on 14 sts.

Row 1: Knit.

Row 2: Inc 1 st at each end of next row (16 sts).

Row 3: Knit.

Row 4: Inc 1 st at each end of next row (18 sts).

Work another 4 rows without shaping.

Row 9: Sl1, K1, psso, K to last 2 sts, K2tog.

Next and foll even rows: Knit.

Rep last 2 rows until 6 sts rem.

Break off yarn, thread through rem sts, pull up tightly and fasten off.

Pin to elephant's head at a slightly sideways angle and

stitch in place. Stitch the cast-on edge to the head.

Tail

Plait (braid) three strands of 4-ply yarn together for 5 cm (2 in). Knot and fray the ends to make a little tassel. Stitch to the elephant's bottom.

Ma Elephant

Body

Cast on 8 sts (3, 2, 3). Join into a ring being careful not to twist the sts.

Round 1: Knit.

Round 2: Inc in each st (16 sts).

Rounds 3 and 4: Knit.

Round 5: *K1, inc in next st, rep from * to end of round (24 sts).

Rounds 6 and 7: Knit.

Round 8: *K2, inc in next st, rep from * to end of round (32 sts).

Rounds 9–11: Knit.

Round 12: *K3, inc in next st, rep from * to end of round (40 sts).

Rounds 13–32: Knit.

Round 33: *K3, Sl1, K1, psso, rep from * to end of round (32 sts).

Rounds 34–36: Knit.

Round 37: *K2, Sl1, K1, psso, rep from * to end of round (24 sts).

Rounds 38–39: Knit.

Round 40: *K4, Sl1, K1, psso, rep from * to end of round (20 sts).

Rounds 41–43: Knit.

Round 44: *K3, Sl1, K1, psso, rep from * to end of round (16 sts).

Work another 25 rounds st st (every row knit) for the trunk.

Picot round: K1, *yfwd, K2tog, rep from * to last st, K1. Work another 5 rounds knit.

At this point stuff the elephant firmly through the trunk.

Note: The knitting is still on the needles but if you proceed further you won't be able to stuff the shape. Do not overfill the trunk, it should be bendy.

*K2tog rep from * to end of round.

Next round: *K2tog, rep from * to end of round. Break off yarn, thread through rem sts, pull up tightly and fold the end of the trunk in at the picot edge.

Ears

Make 2

Cast on 12 sts.

Row 1 and all odd rows: Knit.

Row 2: Inc 1 st at each end of row.

Row 4: K1, M1, knit to last st, M1, K1.

Row 6: Sl1, K1, psso, K to last 2 sts, K2tog.

Rep last 2 rows until 4 sts rem.

Cast off.

Pin the cast-on edge of the ears to the elephant's head at a slightly sideways angle and stitch in place.

Legs

Make 4

Cast on 12 sts.

Work 6 rows st st.

Row 7: K2tog all across.

Break off yarn, thread through rem sts, pull up tightly and fasten off.

With RS facing, sew row ends together. Turn RS out. Stuff firmly with polyester toy filling. Pin to underside of elephant and stitch in position all around.

Tail

Plait three strands of 4-ply yarn together for 4 cm (1¼ in). Knot and fray the ends to make a little tassel. Stitch to the elephant's bottom.

Baby Elephant
Body

Using 4 x 2.25 mm knitting needles, and 4-ply yarn, cast on 8 sts (3, 2, 3). Join into a ring being careful not to twist the sts.

Round 1: Knit.

Round 2: Inc in each st (16 sts).

Rounds 3 and 4: Knit.

Round 5: *K1, inc in next st, rep from * to end of round (24 sts).

Rounds 6 and 7: Knit.

Round 5: *K2, inc in next st, rep from * to end of round (32 sts).

Work another 15 rounds st st (every round knit).

Round 21: *K2, Sl1, K1, psso, rep from * to end of round.

Rounds 22 and 23: Knit.

Round 24: *K4, Sl1, K1, psso, rep from * to end of round (20 sts).

Rounds 25–27: Knit.

Round 28: *K2, Sl1, K1, psso, rep from * to end of round (14 sts).

Work another 15 rounds st st without further shaping for trunk.

Picot round: K1, *yfwd, K2tog, rep from * to last st, K1.

Rounds 45–49: Knit.

At this point stuff the elephant firmly through the trunk. The knitting is on the needles, but if you proceed any further you won't be able to stuff the shape. Do not overfill the trunk.

*K2tog rep from * to end of round.

Next round: *K2tog, rep from * to end of round. Break off yarn, thread through rem sts, pull up tightly and fold the end of the trunk inside itself at the picot edge.

Legs

Make 4

Cast on 10 sts.

Work 5 rows st st.

Row 6: K2tog all across.

Break off yarn, thread through rem sts, pull up tightly and fasten off.

With RS facing, sew row ends together. Turn RS out. Stuff firmly with polyester toy filling. Pin to underside of elephant and stitch in place.

Ears

Make 2

Cast on 8 sts.

Row 1: Knit.

Row 2: K1, inc in next st, knit to last 2 sts, inc in next st, K1.

Row 3: Knit.

Rep last 2 rows once.

Knit 2 rows garter st.

Next row: Sl1, K1, psso, K to last 2 sts, K2tog.

Next row: Knit.

Rep last 2 rows until 4 sts rem.

Break off yarn, thread through rem sts, pull up tightly and fasten off.

Pin the cast-on edge to the elephant's head at a slightly sideways angle and stitch in place.

Tail

Plait three strands of yarn together for 3 cm (1¼ in). Knot and fray the ends to make a little tassel. Stitch to elephant's bottom.

Grandpa Elephant

Grandpa is the oldest and wisest elephant of the family. He has a massive body and the shortest legs, but being so old means he has a long memory and having the largest ears means he hears everything.

MATERIALS

25 g (1 oz) dark grey 4-ply (fingering/sports weight) yarn
Small amount of bright blue 4-ply (fingering/sports weight) yarn, for the scarf
Black stranded embroidery cotton, for the eyes
Wool needle, for sewing up
Sewing needle
Polyester toy filling
Set of 2 mm (UK 14/US 0) knitting needles
Pair of 2.25 mm (UK 13/US 1) knitting needles

MEASUREMENTS

12 cm (4¾ in) tall

Body

Using 4 x 2 mm double-pointed knitting needles and dark grey, cast on 9 sts (3, 3, 3). Join into a ring, being careful not to twist the sts.

Round 1: Knit 1.

Round 2: Inc in every st (18 sts).

Rounds 3 and 4: Knit.

Round 5: Inc in every st (36 sts).

Rounds 6–8: Knit.

Round 9: *K2, inc in next st, rep from * to end of round (48 sts).

Rounds 10–12: Knit.

Round 13: *K2, inc in next st, rep from * to end of round (64 sts).

Rounds 14–15: Knit.

Round 16: Inc 3 sts evenly across needle 1, 2 sts across needle 2, and 3 sts across needle 3 (72 sts).

Work another 2.5 cm (1 in) st st without shaping.

Dec round 1: *K2, K2tog rep from * to end of round (54 sts).

Rounds 2 and 3: Knit.

Round 4: *Sl1, K1, psso, K4, K2tog, rep from * to end of round (36 sts).

Work another 2 cm (¾ in) without further shaping.

Next round: *K4, K2tog, rep from * to end of round.

Stuff the body very firmly ensuring a good pear shape.

Next round: Knit.

Next round: *K2, K2tog, rep from * to end of round.

Next round: Knit.

Add more stuffing, if needed.

Next round: *K1, K2tog, rep from * to end of round.

Next round: *K2 tog, rep all round.

Check stuffing is very firm.

Break off yarn, thread through rem sts, pull up tightly and fasten off.

Head

Using 4 x 2 mm double-pointed knitting needles and dark grey, cast on 5 sts.

Row 1: Inc in each st (10 sts).

Beg with a purl row, work st st for 8 rows, inc 1st at each end of the 8th row.

Work another 9 rows st st.

Row 19: K1, *M1, K1, rep from * to end (23 sts).

Rows 20–22: St st.

Row 23: K5, (M1, K1 13 times), K5 (36 sts).

Work another 19 rows st st.

Row 33: *K1, K2tog, rep from * to end (24 sts).

Row 34: *K2tog, rep from * to end.

Break off yarn, thread through rem sts, pull up tightly and fasten off.

Gather up the cast-on sts and join the trunk seam. Turn RS out. Stuff the trunk firmly. Join the row ends forming the under-head seam. Stuff very firmly to make a rounded shape. Attach the head to the body at the top of the pear shape but not sitting right on top. The elephant will have a humped back.

Eyes

Mark the eye positions above the top of the trunk and 1.5 cm (½ in) apart. Work a French knot for each eye using three strands of black embroidery cotton.

Tail

Using 2 x 2 mm double-pointed knitting needles and dark grey, cast on 3 sts. Work an I-cord for 5 cm (2 in). Fasten off. Make a tassel with a few extra strands of grey and stitch it on to the end of the tail. Stitch the other end to the elephant's bottom.

Legs

Make 4

Using 2 x 2 mm double-pointed knitting needles and yarn, cast on 16 sts.

Work 8 rows st st.

Next row: K2tog all across row.

Break off yarn, thread through rem sts, pull up tightly and fasten off.

With RS facing, sew row ends together. Turn RS out. Stuff firmly with polyester toy filling.

Mark the leg placement on the elephant's tummy. The back legs will be level with the bottom of the elephant and 4 cm (1¾ in) apart. The front legs are placed 3 cm (1¼ in) above the back legs and the same distance apart. Stitch firmly in place.

Scarf

Using 2.25 mm knitting needles and blue, cast on 55 sts. Work 2 rows garter st. Cast off.

Darn in all ends, knot around the elephant's neck.

Fantastic Fish

These fish are small in scale, but are a perfect size to decorate with beads. Make a shoal with a fantastic array of beaded patterns. These fish are unsuitable for very small children when decorated with beads but you could leave them plain and they would still look good.

MATERIALS

Oddments of 4-ply (fingering/sports weight) yarn in shades of blue
Pair of 2 mm (UK 14/US 0) knitting needles
Wool needle, for sewing up
Polyester toy filling
Blue sequins
Clear sequins
Bright blue glass seed beads
Dark blue glass seed beads
Beading needle
Polyester thread or beading thread
Black stranded embroidery cotton, for the features
Erasable marker pen

MEASUREMENTS

9 cm (3½ in) long

NOTE

Each fish body is made in two pieces, with the tail knitted and sewn in place once the body is complete. The fins are attached last.

Body

Using blue yarn, cast on 12 sts.

Work in st st for 10 rows.

Row 11: K3, *M1, K3 rep from * to end (15 sts).

Work another 5 rows st st beg with a purl row.

Row 17: K3, *M1, K3 rep from * to end (19 sts).

Work another 5 rows st st, beg with a purl row.

Row 23: K3, *M1, K1 rep from * to last 3 sts, K3 (32 sts).

Work another 13 rows st st, beg with a purl row.

Row 37: *K2, K2tog, rep from * to end.

Row 38: Purl.

Row 39: *K1, K2tog, rep from * to end (16 sts).

Row 40: Purl.

Row 41: K2tog all across.

Break off yarn, thread through rem sts, pull up tightly
and fasten off.

With RS together, join seam, leaving a gap for turning.
Turn right side out and stuff firmly. Stitch seam closed.
Run a gathering thread around the cast-on edge and
pull up firmly so that this opening is closed. It will fit
into the fish tail.

Using the erasable marker pen, mark the position of
the eyes on each side of the face and draw in a smiling
mouth. Make French knot eyes using three strands of
black embroidery cotton. Work the mouth in stem stitch
using three strands of black embroidery cotton. Finish
off the ends inside the body of the fish.

Tail

Using blue yarn, cast on 8 sts.

Row 1: Purl.

Starting with a knit row and working in st st, inc 1 st at
the beg of next 10 rows until there are 18 sts.

Row 11: K5, (K2tog four times), K5 (14 sts).

Row 12: Purl

Row 13: K5, inc 1 st in each of the next 4 sts, K5 (18 sts).

Row 14: Dec 1 st at beg of next and every foll row until 8 sts rem.

Work 1 more row.

Cast off.

With RS together, fold the tail in half and sew side edges together. Turn RS out and push out the points of the tail using a blunt pencil. Position the tail over the end of the body and stitch in place all around.

Fins

Make 2

Using blue yarn, cast on 8 sts.

Row 1: Purl.

Row 2: K3, inc 1 st in each of the next 2 sts, K3 (10 sts).

Beg with a purl row, work 5 rows st st.

Row 8: K2tog all across.

Break off yarn, thread through rem sts, pull up tightly and fasten off.

The fin is very small so it is easier to sew it together with WS facing. The cast-on edges of the fins are stitched to the fish. Place them half way down the body and slightly lower than the eye. Darn in any loose ends.

Beading

The tail is covered with sequins and glass beads. Thread the beading needle with a length of polyester or beading thread and knot firmly in place using a couple of very small stitches on the fish tail. Bring the needle up through a sequin and a bead and then down the side of the bead and back through the sequin. Place the next sequin very close and repeat the process until the top of the tail is covered in sequins and beads. The top half of the body is beaded up to the point where the fins are attached. Ensure that the beads are sewn on very firmly. Sew beads randomly on the head.

Herbert the Hippo

This little chap is quite adorable. He is a little bit larger than some of the miniature animals but still takes less than 50 g (1¾ oz) of yarn to knit. You could knit him in any colour you like, but I love this dark grey sock yarn.

MATERIALS

50 g (1¾ oz) 4-ply (fingering/sports weight) dark grey yarn
Small amount of white 4-ply (fingering/sports weight) yarn, for the teeth
Black stranded embroidery cotton
White stranded embroidery cotton
Sewing needle
Pair of 2 mm (UK 14/US 0) knitting needles
Polyester toy filling
Wool needle, for sewing up

TENSION

The pieces that make up the hippo are knitted on needles much smaller than you would generally use for the ply of yarn. This is to give a very firm fabric. If you are a tight knitter you could try using 2.25 mm (UK 13/US 1) knitting needles instead.

Body

Using dark grey, cast on 7 sts.

Rows 1, 3 and 5: Purl.

Row 2: Inc in every st (14 sts).

Row 4: Inc in every st (28 sts).

Row 6: Inc in every st (56 sts).

Work another 39 rows st st without shaping, ending with a purl row.

Row 46: *K2tog, rep from * to end.

Row 47: Purl.

Rep last two rows until 7 sts rem.

Break off yarn. Thread through rem sts, pull up tightly and fasten off.

With RS tog, join the central body seam. Turn RS out and fill firmly with polyester toy filling. Make sure the hippo has a sturdy round shape. Close the neck opening.

Head

Using dark grey, cast on 60 sts.

Beg with a knit row, work 15 rows st st.

Row 16: *K2tog, rep from * to end (30 sts).

Work another 12 rows st st.

Row 29: K7, inc in each of next 16 sts, K7 (46 sts).

Work another 5 rows st st.

Row 35: K7, (K2tog 16 times), K7 (30 sts).

Row 36: Purl.

Row 37: K2tog all across row.

Cast off.

Stitch the head seam closed. Fill the head firmly but leave the head open. Pin on to the body, matching seams and stitch in place all round.

Underside of mouth

Using dark grey yarn, cast on 15 sts.

Beg with a knit row, work 6 rows st st.

Row 7: Dec 1 st at each end of next 4 rows (7 sts).

Row 8: Inc 1 st at each end of next 4 rows (15 sts)

Work another 6 rows st st without further shaping.

Cast off.

Fold in half and join the edges. Centre under the nose and stitch in place.

Tail

Using dark grey yarn, cast on 7 sts. Cast off. Sew the tail to the hippo's bottom.

Legs

Make 4

Using dark grey yarn, cast on 20 sts.

Work 16 rows st st, beg with a knit row.

Row 17: Break off yarn. Thread through rem sts, pull up tightly and fasten off.

With RS tog, sew side seam. Turn right side out and fill firmly with polyester toy filling. Do not close the top of the leg. Pin in place on the under-body of the hippo and using small stitches, sew in place all around the top of the leg.

Ears

Using dark grey yarn, cast on 6 sts.

Work 4 rows st st, beg with a knit row.

Row 5: Dec 1 st at each end of the next row (4 sts).

Row 6: Inc 1st at each end of the next row (6 sts).

Work another 4 rows st st without further shaping.

Cast off.

Fold the ears together with WS facing. Using very small stitches, sew the sides. Make a little pleat in the base of each ear and stitch across so the pleat is held in place. Pin on the back of the hippo's head and stitch in place.

Eyes

Using dark grey yarn, cast on 20 sts.

Work 4 rows st st, beg with a knit row.

Row 5: K2tog all across.

Row 6: P2tog all across.

Row 7: Break off yarn. Thread through rem sts, pull up tightly and fasten off.

Stitch side seam and fill firmly with polyester toy filling. Run a gathering thread around the cast-on edge and draw closed. Pin on to the hippo's head, then stitch in position.

Using three strands of white embroidery cotton, embroider a French knot on each eye.

Teeth

Make 2

Using knitting needles and six strands of white embroidery cotton, cast on 4 sts. Knit 4 rows st st. Cast off.

Roll each tooth into a cylinder and stitch down the long end. It is easier to do this with just one strand of embroidery cotton.

Darn in any loose ends. Stitch one tooth to the upper side of the hippo's jaw.

Leander the Lion

Soft and squishy and with his magnificent mane of golden hair, this little lion cub is sure to be cherished by any big cat-lover. Why not make a pride of lions and use them to ornament a sun-baked windowsill in a child's bedroom?

MATERIALS

Small amount (less than 25 g/1 oz) light brown 4-ply (fingering/sports weight) yarn
Small amount of gold eyelash yarn, for the mane and tail tassel
Brown stranded embroidery cotton, for the features
Polyester toy filling
Pair of 2.25 mm (UK 13/US 1) knitting needles
Wool needle, for sewing up
Sewing needle

MEASUREMENTS

12 cm (4¾ in) tall

Body

Using light brown yarn, cast on 7 sts.

Row 1: *K1, yfwd, rep from * to last st, K1 (13 sts).

Row 2: Purl.

Row 3: K1, *yfwd, K2 rep from * to end (19 sts).

Row 4: Purl.

Rep last 2 rows once (28 sts) ending inc row with K1 (29 sts).

Row 7: K3*, yfwd, K3, rep from * to last 4 sts, K4 (36 sts)**

Work 28 rows st st beg with a knit row.

Row 36: K3,* K2tog, K2, rep from * to last 3 sts, K3.

Row 37: Purl.

Row 38: K1, *K2tog, K1, rep from * to last 2 sts, K2.

Row 39: Purl.

Row 40: K2tog all across.

Break off yarn. Thread through rem sts, pull up tightly and fasten off.

With RS tog, sew centre back seam two-thirds of the way closed. Turn RS out. Stuff the body firmly with polyester toy filling. Stitch rest of seam closed.

Head

Using light brown yarn, cast on 5 sts.

Row 1: Purl.

Row 2: Inc in every st (10 sts).

Row 3: Purl.

Row 4: Inc in every st to end (20 sts).

Row 5: Purl.

Row 6: *Inc in next st, K1, rep from * to end (30 sts).

Work another 22 rows st st, beg with a purl row.

Row 29: *K1, K2tog, rep from * to end (20 sts).

Row 30: Purl.

Row 31: *K1, K2tog, rep from * to last 2 sts, K2.

Row 32: Purl.

Row 33: K2tog all across.

Break off yarn, thread through rem sts, pull up tightly and fasten off.

With RS tog, sew centre back head seam two-thirds of the way closed. Turn RS out. Stuff the head firmly with polyester toy filling. Stitch closed the remainder of the seam.

Muzzle

Using light brown, cast on 7 sts.

Row 1: Inc in first st, K1, inc in next st, knit to last 3 sts, inc in next st, K1, inc in last st (11 sts).

Beg with a purl row, work 7 rows st st.

Row 9: K2tog all across.

Break off yarn, thread through rem sts, pull up tightly and fasten off.

Run a gathering thread around the muzzle and draw up to form a rounded shape. Stuff with a tiny amount of polyester toy filling. Stitch on to lion's head so that the base of the muzzle is in the chin area. Use three strands of brown embroidery cotton and stem stitch to embroider the nose features.

Mane

Using golden eyelash yarn, cast on 60 sts.

Knit 1 row.

Cast off.

Ears

Make 2

Using light brown, cast on 4 sts.

Row 1: K2, M1, K2.

Row 2: Purl.

Row 3: K3, M1, K3 (7 sts)

Row 4: Purl.

Row 5: K2tog, K3, K2tog.

Row 6: Purl.

Row 7: K2tog, K1, K2tog.

Row 8: Purl.

Row 9: Knit.

Row 10: K2tog all across.

Break off yarn, thread through rem sts, pull up tightly and fasten off.

Fold ear in half, WS tog and stitch sides tog. Create a tiny pleat at the lower edge so that each ear points forwards. Pin to the top of the lion's head, widely spaced apart and stitch in place.

Pin the strip of mane in front of one ear, and around the back of the head, winding in concentric circles, so that it completely covers the back of the head. Pin in position as you go. Sew in place with polyester thread.

Sew the eyes with brown embroidery cotton using French knots, just above and to each side of the muzzle. Finally stitch the head firmly to the top of the body.

Front Legs

Make 2

Using light brown yarn, cast on 12 sts.

Row 1: Knit, inc in first and last st (14 sts).

Work another 5 rows beg with a purl row.

Row 7: K4, (K2tog 3 times), K4 (11 sts).

Row 8: P2tog at beg and end of row (9 sts).

Work another 20 rows st st without shaping.

Row 29: Sl1, K1, psso, knit to last 2 sts, K2tog.

Row 30: Purl.

Row 31: K1, K2tog all across.

Break off yarn, thread through rem sts, pull up tightly and fasten off.

With RS facing, sew part way up the seam using invisible stitches. (The legs are small so it is difficult to turn them.) Stuff the legs firmly and attach to the shoulders.

Back Legs

Make 2

Using light brown yarn, cast on 11 sts.

Row 1: Knit, inc 1 st at beg and end of row (13 sts).

Work another 5 rows st st beg with a purl row.

Row 7: (Sl1, K1, psso three times), K3, (K2tog three times), K1.

Work another 7 rows st st.

Row 15: Sl1, K1, psso, knit to last 3 sts, K2tog, K1.

Row 16: Purl.

Break off yarn, thread through rem sts, pull up tightly and fasten off.

Stitch seam tog for two-thirds of the way and then firmly stuff the legs. Position on the underside of the lion so that he is able to sit up on his back legs, pin and stitch in place.

Tail

Using light brown yarn, cast on 8 sts.

Row 1: Knit.

Row 2: Purl.

Row 3: K2tog, knit to end.

Row 4: Purl.

Row 5: K5, K2tog.

Rows 6–8: St st.

Row 9: K2tog, K4.

Work another 6 rows st st,

Row 16: K1, K2tog all across. Break off yarn, thread through rem sts, pull up tightly and fasten off.

Cut a few lengths of eyelash yarn for the tassel. These will be enclosed inside the end of the tail once the side seam is sewn. Using mattress stitch, sew down the length of the tail, catching in the tassel threads toward the end. Secure the end firmly. Sew the other end to the lion's bottom. Trim the tassel to the desired length.

Bertie Bear

Who doesn't love a teddy bear? This little bear can sit or stand and is just the right size to be carried around in a pocket. For a slightly larger bear use a thicker yarn.

MATERIALS

25 g (1 oz) of brown 4-ply (fingering/sports weight) yarn, for the bear
Pair of 2 mm (UK 14/US 0) knitting needles
Wool needle, for sewing up
Polyester toy filling
Long doll needle, for attaching arms and legs
Two 6 mm (¼ in) black beads, for the eyes
Black stranded embroidery cotton, for the nose
Pins

Body

Cast on 16 sts for the neck edge.

Row 1: Purl.

Row 2: K1, inc in every st to end (31 sts).

Work 3 rows st st.

Row 6: K8, M1, K13, M1, K8 (33 sts).

Work another 11 rows st st.

Row 18: K15, M1, K3, M1, K15 (35 sts).

Work 3 rows st st.

Row 22: K3, M1, K1, M1, K27, M1, K1, M1, K3 (39 sts).

Row 23: Purl.

Row 24: K16, Sl1, K1, psso, K3, K2tog, K16 (37 sts).

Work 5 rows st st.

Row 30: K15, Sl1, K1, psso, K3, K2tog, K15 (35 sts).

Work 3 rows st st.

Row 34: K1, (K2tog all across) (18 sts).

Row 35: Purl.

Row 36: K2tog all across.

Break off yarn, thread through rem sts, pull up tightly and fasten off.

Using mattress st, sew most of centre back seam. Leave neck edge open and fill very firmly with polyester toy filling to give a round shape. Finish closing back seam, but leave neck edge open.

Head

Cast on 7 sts.

Row 1: Purl.

Row 2: K1, inc in every st to end of row (13 sts).

Row 3: Purl.

Row 4: K1, inc in every st to end of row (25 sts).

Work 5 rows st st.

Row 10: (K2, M1 four times), K9, (M1, K2 four times) (33 sts).

Work another 13 rows st st.

Row 24: K8, (K2tog twice), K9, (Sl1, K1, psso twice), K8

(29 sts).

Row 25: Purl.

Row 26: K1, (K2tog 6 times), K3, (Sl1, K1, psso 6 times), K1 (17 sts).

Work another 3 rows st st.

Row 26: K1, K2tog all across to end of row (9 sts).

Break off yarn, thread through rem sts, pull up tightly and fasten off.

Sew up seam beg at cast-on end, which is the back of the head. Leave an opening for stuffing. Fill firmly with polyester toy filling. Once you are happy with the shape of the head, close the seam. Position on top of the body and pin in place using glass-headed pins. Stitch firmly to the open neck edge at the top of the body.

Ears

Make 2

Cast on 5 sts.

Row 1: Knit.

Row 2: K1, M1 in next st, K1, M1 in next st, K1 (7 sts).

Row 3: Knit.

Row 4: K1, M1 in next st, K3, M1 in next st, K1 (9 sts).

Row 5: Knit.

Cast off.

The cast-off edge is the edge that attaches to the head. Run a gathering thread along this edge so that you can form a curved shape.

Pin the ears to the head and when you are happy with their placement, stitch in place.

Legs

Make 2

Beginning at bottom edge of foot, cast on 10 sts.

Row 1: Purl.

Row 2: K1, inc in every st to the end (19 sts).

Row 3: Purl.

Row 4: K4, (M1 in next st, K2 five times) (24 sts).

Work 5 rows st st beg with a purl row.

Row 10: K8, (Sl1, K1, psso twice), (K2tog twice), K8 (20 sts).

Row 11: P6, (P2tog twice), (P2togtbl twice), P6 (16 sts).

Row 12: K7, K2tog, K7 (15 sts).

Row 13: Knit.

Row 14: Purl.

Row 15: Knit.

Row 16: K2, M1 in next st, K10, M1 in next st, K1 (17 sts).

Work another 11 rows st st without shaping.

Row 28: K1, K2tog all across.

Break off yarn, thread through rem sts, pull up tightly and fasten off.

As the pieces are very small it is easier to sew the seam with WS tog. Starting at the bottom of the foot, and using very small stitches, close the seam. When the seam is three-quarters sewn, stuff the leg with polyester toy filling. Use the blunt end of a pencil to help push the stuffing all the way to the toe. Finish sewing the seam.

Right Arm

Cast on 6 sts, beg at the paw.

Row 1: Purl.

Row 2: K1, inc in every st to end (11 sts).

Row 3: Purl.

Row 4: K2, (M1 twice), K3, (M1, twice) K2 (15 sts)

Knit 5 rows st st beg with a purl row.

Row 10: K1, (Sl1, K1, psso) twice, (K2tog) twice, K6 (11 sts).

Work another 7 rows st st without shaping.

Row 18: K5, M1, K3, M1, K3 (13 sts).

Work another 9 rows st st without shaping.

Row 28: K1, K2tog all across.

Make up as for foot, beg at tip of paw.

Left Arm

Cast on 6 sts, beg at paw.

Row 1: Purl.

Row 2: K1, inc in every st to end (11 sts).

Row 3: Purl.

Row 4: (K2, M1) twice, K3, (M1, K2) twice (15 sts).

Work 5 rows st st beg with a purl row.

Row 10: K6, (Sl1, K1, psso) twice, (K2tog) twice, K1 (11 sts).

Work another 7 rows st st without shaping.

Row 18: K5, M1, K3, M1, K3 (13 sts).

Work another 9 rows st st without shaping.

Row 28: K1, K2tog all across.

Make up as for foot, beg at tip of paw.

Assembling the Bear

Place left and right arms at each side of the body, and level with the top of the body. Use matching yarn to sew right through the arm and the body. Take several stitches through and pull firmly. The arm should sit flat against the body, but will still be able to move. Repeat for the other side.

Use the same method for attaching the legs, ensuring that you have them positioned evenly.

Embroider the nose using three strands of black embroidery cotton and using satin stitch. Give the teddy a smiley mouth using stem stitch. Sew on the black beads for eyes using matching black polyester thread.

Little Bluebird of Happiness

This fun little bird will add a cheery note to any surface.
The simple shape is quick and easy to knit, and is decorated
with a fancy top knot and yellow feet and beak.

MATERIALS

Small amount (less than 25 g/1 oz) royal blue 4-ply
(fingering/sports weight) yarn
Small amount of contrast 4-ply (fingering/sports weight)
yarn, for the beak and feet
Pair of 2 mm (UK 14/US 0) knitting needles
Wool needle, for sewing up
Polyester toy filling
2 tiny black beads, for the eyes
Black stranded embroidery cotton (optional)
Sewing needle
Beading thread or polyester thread

MEASUREMENTS

6 cm (2¼ in) tall

Body

Using royal blue, cast on 7 sts.

Row 1: *K1, yfwd, rep from * to end (13 sts).

Row 2: Purl.

Row 3: K1, *yfwd , K2 rep from * to end (19 sts).

Row 4: Purl.

Rep rows 3 and 4 once, ending inc row with K1 (28 sts).

Row 7: Knit.

Row 8: Purl.

Work another 16 rows st st.

Row 25: K3, *K2tog, K2, rep from * to last st, K1.

Row 26: Purl.

Row 27: K2, *K2tog, K1, rep from * to last 2 sts, K2.

Row 28: Purl.

Row 29: K1, *K2tog all across.

Break off yarn, thread through rem sts, pull up tightly and fasten off.

With RS tog, sew two-thirds of the back seam. Turn RS out. Firmly stuff the body to achieve an oval shape. Use mattress st to close the seam.

Wings

Make 2

Using royal blue yarn, cast on 10 sts.

Row 1: Purl.

Row 1: Inc in every st (20 sts).

Beg with a knit row, dec 1 st at each end of every row until 4 sts rem.

Break off yarn, thread through rem sts, pull up tightly and fasten off.

With WS tog, sew row ends together and then stitch across cast-on stitches. Sew wings to body 1.5 cm (⁵/₈ in) down from top of head.

Tail Feathers

Using royal blue yarn, cast on 5 sts.
Row 1: Purl.
Row 1: Inc in every st (10 sts).
Beg with a knit row, dec 1 st at each end of every row until 2 sts rem.
Break off yarn, thread through rem sts, pull up tightly and fasten off.
With WS tog, sew row ends together and then stitch across cast-on stitches. Sew tail feathers to rear of bird on centre back seam 1 cm (^{3}/$_8$ in) up from the base.

Feet

Make 2
Using yellow yarn, cast on 3 sts.
Row 1: Inc into every st (6 sts).
Beg with a purl row, work 6 rows st st.
Next row: (K2tog, yrn) twice, K2tog (5 sts).
Beg with a knit row, work 4 rows st st.
Cast off.
Sew the cast-on and cast-off edges of the foot together and then stitch to the underside of the bird's body.

Beak

Using yellow yarn, cast on 1 st.
Row 1: Knit into the front, back and front of st (3 sts).
Row 2: Purl.
Row 3: Inc in first and last st (5 sts).
Row 4: Purl.
Row 5: Inc in first and last st (7 sts).
Row 6: Purl.
Cast off.
Fold beak in half, WS facing. Stitch the edges together and then sew on to the bird between the eyes, with the point facing down toward the toes.

Top Knot

Take a few looped strands of the blue yarn and stitch in place on top of the bird's head, catching them in place with small stitches.

Kitty Cat

This adorable little kitten is knitted, stuffed and needle-felted all over to give a fuzzy soft appearance. This is a challenging project to make and requires a little patience, but the results, for the cat lover, are worth it.

MATERIALS

Small amount of variegated grey 4-ply (fingering/sports weight) yarn

Small amount of grey contrast 4-ply (fingering/sports weight) yarn, for tummy and ears

Pair of 2 mm (UK 14/US 0) knitting needles

Wool needle, for sewing up

Polyester toy filling

Green stranded embroidery cotton

Black stranded embroidery cotton

Black and cream merino needle-felting wool

Needle-felting needle

Sewing needle

Erasable marker pen

TENSION

2 mm needles will create a very firm fabric when used with 4-ply yarn. This is intentional so that you have a strong base on which to needle felt. If you are a tight knitter, try using 2.25 mm (UK 13/US 1) knitting needles instead.

Head and Body

Using variegated grey yarn, cast on 20 sts.

Beg with a knit row, work 16 rows st st.

Row 17: Inc in first st, K7, K2tog, knit to last st, inc (20 sts).

Row 18: Purl.

Rep last 2 rows twice more. Mark both ends of row.

Row 21: Inc into each of first 2 sts, K6, inc into each of next 4 sts, knit to last 2 sts, inc into each of next 2 sts (28 sts).

Row 22: Purl.

Row 23: Inc into each of first 2 sts, K10, inc into each of next 4 sts, K to last 2 sts, inc into each of next 2 sts (36 sts).

Work another 5 rows st st.

Row 29: ((K2tog twice), K10, (K2tog twice) twice) (28 sts).

Row 30: Purl.

Row 31: ((K2tog twice), K6, (K2tog twice) twice) (20 sts).

Row 32: Purl.

Cast off.

With WS facing, fold piece in half, matching markers. Join the seam from the top of the head to the spot where the marker is placed. Use very small, closely placed stitches.

Tummy

Using grey contrast yarn, cast on 3 sts.

Work 2 rows st st.

Row 3 and foll odd rows: Inc 1 st at each end of row until there are 11 sts.

Row 4 and all even rows: Purl.

Next and foll alt knit rows: Dec 1 st at each end of row until 3 sts rem.

Work another 3 rows without shaping.

Next row: Sl1, K2tog, psso.

Fasten off.

With WS together, match the pointed neck end of the tummy piece to the coloured marker on the body piece. Using matching yarn, join side of the tummy piece down the front of the body and along the base to the second point. Stuff the kitten, until shape is rounded. Finish sewing up along the other side of the tummy to the neck marker.

Front Legs

Make 2

Using variegated yarn, cast on 4 sts.

Row 1: Purl.

Row 2: Inc in each st (8 sts).

Work another 19 rows st st without shaping.

Cast off.

Fold leg in half with WS tog. When the seam is sewn halfway, push some tiny pieces of polyester toy filling into the toe section using a blunt pencil. Finish sewing the seam and use more tiny pieces of polyester filling to stuff the leg. Ladder stitch the front legs to the kitten, bending the paw sections (cast-on edge) upward as you sew.

Back Legs

Make 2

Using variegated grey yarn, cast on 4 sts.

Row 1: Purl.

Row 2: Inc in each st (8 sts).

Work another 13 rows st st.

Cast off.

Make up back legs as for front legs but do not bend up. Sew in place to the sides of the kitten's body so that the kitten can sit in a stable position.

Tail

Using variegated grey yarn, cast on 8 sts.

Beg with a knit row, work 26 rows st st.

Row 27: K2tog four times.

Break off yarn, thread through rem sts, pull up tightly and fasten off.

With WS tog, stitch along row ends, stuffing the tail very lightly as you go. Attach the cast-off end to the kitten.

Ears

Make 4

Using grey contrast yarn, cast on 6 sts.

Work 4 rows st st beg with a knit row.

Row 5: Sl1, K1, psso, K2, K2tog.

Row 6: Purl.

Row 7: Sl1, K1, psso, K2tog.

Row 8: Purl.

Row 9: Sl1, K1, psso.

Fasten off.

With RS tog, stitch around the outside of a pair of ears. Darn in any loose ends. Pin the ears to the kitten and when you are happy with the position, stitch in place. It can be helpful to make a small pleat in the base of each ear before attaching it to the head of the kitten.

Face

Use a chalk pencil or erasable marker pen to draw on the features. Embroider the eyes using three strands of green embroidery cotton and making a French knot for each eye. The nose is made from three strands of black embroidery cotton and satin stitch.

Needle Felting

Place the kitten on a thick sponge. Take tiny amounts of black and cream needle-felting wool and arrange it on top of the kitten. Stab the felting needle in and out until the kitten is covered in yarn. This is quite a slow process as you need to do each part of the body separately.

Owl Family

The design of this little family of owls is based on a simple oval shape, with little wings and a top knot added to each. Felt eyes, feet and embroidery give the trio of Ma, Pa and Baby their individual and jaunty charm. The largest owl has an I-cord scarf.

MATERIALS

25 g (1 oz) 4-ply (fingering/sports weight) yarn, for each owl

10 cm (4 in) square white felt, for the eyes

5 cm (2 in) square yellow felt, for the large beak, small feet and small beak

5 cm (2 in) square light pink felt, for the medium owl beak

5cm (2 in) square deep pink felt, for the medium owl feet

5 cm (2 in) square grey felt, for the large owl feet

Black stranded embroidery cotton, for the features

Air-soluble marker pen

Embroidery needle

Pair of 2 mm (UK 14/US 0) double-pointed knitting needles

Wool needle, for sewing up

Polyester toy filling

Small amount of red 4-ply (fingering/sports weight) yarn, for large owl's scarf.

Wings

Make 2

Using yarn, cast on 5 sts.

Work 2 rows moss st.

Row 3: P2tog, moss st to end.

Rep this row until 1 st rem.

Fasten off. Darn in loose ends.

Assembling the Owls

Owls are all sewn up in the same manner. With RS tog, stitch the centre-back seam closed for two-thirds of the way. Turn RS out. Stuff firmly with small pieces of polyester toy filling to make a cylindrical shape. Stitch the seam closed, gathering the cast-on edge closed as you sew.

Baby Owl

Using yarn of your choice, cast on 7 sts.

Row 1: *K1, yfwd, rep from * to end (13 sts).

Row 2: Purl.

Row 3: K1, * yfwd , K2 rep from * to end (19 sts).

Row 4: Purl.

Rep last 2 rows once.

Row 7: *K1, P1, rep from * to end.

Row 8: *P1, K1, rep from * to end

Work another 16 rows moss st.

Row 25: K3, *K2tog, K2, rep from * to last st, K1.

Row 26: Purl.

Row 27: K2, *K2tog, K1, rep from * to last 2 sts , K2.

Row 28: Purl.

Row 29: K1, *K2tog all across.

Break off yarn, thread through rem sts, pull up tightly and fasten off.

Stitch the wings to the body aligning the top edge with eye level. Sew across the cast-on edge.

Beak

Trace the template provided and cut out the tracing. Pin to yellow felt for Baby and Pa owls and pink for Ma owl. Fold in half so the point is facing downward. With matching cotton, sew the ends of the beak under using tiny stitches. Sew in place between the eyes.

Foot

Trace the template provided and use to cut out 2 from fabric. Stitch the feet together, then sew to the base of the owl, aligning the middle toe with the beak. Use small stitches and sew through the felt and the knitting for a secure hold.

Eyes

From white felt, for Baby owl, cut two circles each 1 cm ($3/8$ in) diameter. For Ma owl, cut two circles each 1.5 cm ($5/8$ in) diameter. For the Pa owl, cut two circles each 2 cm ($3/4$ in) diameter.

Draw a curved line with an air-soluble marker pen on each eye and work a row of stem stitch over the line using stranded embroidery cotton. Pin in place three-quarters of the way up the owl and with just enough space between to fit the beak. Stitch around each eye using two strands of black embroidery cotton.

Ma Owl

Using 2 mm knitting needles and yarn of choice, cast on 7 sts.

Row 1: *K1, yfwd, rep from * to end (13 sts).

Row 2: Purl.

Row 3: K1, *yfwd , K2 rep from * to end (19 sts).

Row 4: Purl.

Rep last 2 rows once (28 sts).

Row 7: K3, *yfwd, K3, rep from * to last 4 sts, K4 (36 sts)**.

Row 8: *K1, P1, rep from * to end.

Row 9: *P1, K1, rep from * to end.

Rep these 2 rows of moss st another 13 times each.

Row 36: K3, *K2tog, K2, rep from * to last 3 sts.

Row 37: Purl.

Row 38: K1, *K2tog, K1, rep from * to last 2 sts, K2.
Row 39: Purl.
Row 40: Purl. K2tog all across.
Break off yarn. Thread through rem sts pull up tightly and fasten off.

Wings

Make 2
Using 2 mm knitting needles and yarn, cast on 9 sts.
Work 2 rows moss st.
Row 3: P2tog, moss st to end.
Rep this row until 1 st rem.
Fasten off.

Make a foot, eyes and beak following the instructions given for Baby Owl. Assemble Ma Owl following the instructions for Baby Owl.

Pa Owl

Using colour yarn of your choice, work as for Ma Owl up to **.
Row 8: Purl.
Row 9: K2, *yfwd, K4, rep from * to last 3 sts, K3 (46 sts).
Row 10: *K1, P1, rep from * to end.
Row 11: *P1, K1, rep from * to end.
Work another 38 rows moss st.
Dec row: K2, *K2tog, K2, rep from * to last st, K1.
Next row: Purl.
Rep last 2 rows once.
Next row: K2, *K2tog, K1, rep from * to last st, K1.
Next row: Purl.
Repeat last 2 rows once.
Next row: K2tog all across.
Break off yarn. Thread through rem sts, pull up tightly and fasten off.

Wings

Make 2
Using 2 mm knitting needles and yarn, cast on 11 sts.
Work 2 rows moss st.
Row 3: P2tog, moss st to end.
Rep this row until 1 st rem.
Fasten off.

Top Knot

Ma and Pa owls each have a top knot. These are made by making 2 or 3 little loops of yarn and sewing them securely to the top of the head.

Scarf

Using 2 mm double-pointed knitting needles and red 4-ply yarn, cast on 3 sts
Row 1: *Knit, do not turn work, slide sts to end of needle, pull yarn firmly behind work, rep from * until scarf measures 30 cm (12 in).
Next row: Sl1, K2tog, psso, fasten off.
Make a little fringe by cutting lengths of yarn and threading through the ends of the I-cord with a wool needle. Cut them all to the same length and then fray the fibres with the wool needle for a fuzzy effect. Dress on to the owl, under his wings and knotting at the front. Make a foot, eyes and beak following the instructions given for Baby Owl. Assemble Pa Owl following the instructions for Baby Owl.

Owl Pattern Pieces

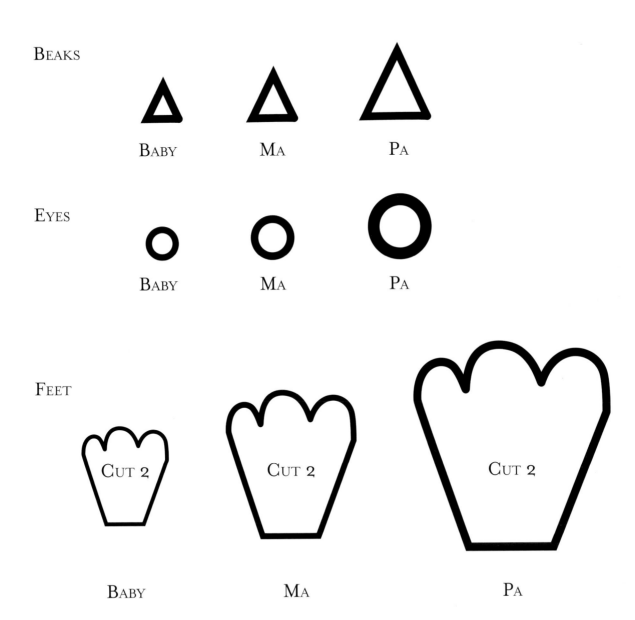

Beaks

Baby Ma Pa

Eyes

Baby Ma Pa

Feet

Cut 2 Cut 2 Cut 2

Baby Ma Pa

Hen in a Nest

Pearl is a tiny chicken knitted from leftover sock wool. She is small enough to sit in the palm of the hand. Here she sits in a nest made from knitted and felted fabric. Be sure to use a yarn that is suitable for felting.

MATERIALS

Small amount (less than 25 g/1 oz) variegated grey 4-ply (fingering/sports weight) sock yarn

Yellow, red and black stranded embroidery cotton

Sewing needle

Polyester toy filling

Wool needle, for sewing up

Pair of 2 mm (UK 14/US 0) knitting needles

Set of 5 mm (UK 6/US 8) double-pointed knitting needles

1 x 50 g (1¾ oz) ball of DK (8-ply) wool suitable for felting

Body

Using 2 mm knitting needles and yarn, cast on 25 sts.
Row 1: Purl.
Row 2: K1, M1, K9, K2tog, K1, Sl1, K1, psso, K9, M1, K1.
Row 2: Purl.
Repeat rows 2 and 3 twice more.
Row 7: K1, M1, K23, M1, K1.
Beg with a purl row, work 5 rows st st.
Row 13: K12, M1, K3, M1, K12.
Row 14: Purl.
Row 15: K13, M1, K3, M1, K13.
Row 16: Purl.
Row 17: (Sl1, K1, psso five times), K4, M1, K3, M1, K4, (K2tog five times).
Row 18: Purl.
Row 19: (Sl1, K1, psso three times), K4, M1, K3, M1, K4, (K2tog three times).
Row 20: Cast off 4 sts, purl to end.
Row 21: Cast off 4 sts, K3, M1, K3, M1, K4.
Row 22: Purl.
Row 23: Knit.
Row 24: P1, *P2tog, rep from * to end.
Break off yarn, thread through rem sts, pull up tightly and fasten off.
Garter st side will be facing out. Sew up the centre seam, which will form the tummy, stuffing the body firmly as you go.

Wings

Make 2
Using 2 mm knitting needles and yarn, cast on 11 sts.
Work in garter st throughout.
Knit 3 rows.
Row 4: Beg wing shaping, K1, Sl1, K1, psso, K to end.
Repeat this row until 3 sts rem.

Break off yarn, thread through rem sts, pull up tightly and fasten off.
    Fold wing in half and stitch closed. Place one wing at each side of the chicken and stitch into position. The wide end of the wing faces the rear end of the chicken.

Beak and Crest

Using a small amount of yellow yarn, embroider the beak using a few short stitches. To make the chicken's red crest. Make a straight stitch on top of the head using red yarn. Do not make it too tight. Buttonhole this straight stitch to give it a slightly curly effect.

Nest

Using set of 5 mm double-pointed knitting needles and felting yarn, cast on 45 sts (15, 15, 15). Join into a ring, taking care not to twist the stitches.
Knit 15 rounds.
Shape Base
Round 1: *K2tog, K7, rep from * to end of round.
Round 2: *K2tog, K6, rep from * to end of round.
Round 3: *K2tog, K5 rep from * to end of round.
Round 4: *K2tog, K4, rep from * to end of round.
Round 5: *K2tog, K3, rep from * to end of round.
Round 6: *K2tog, K2, rep from * to end of round.
Round 7: *K2tog, K1, rep from * to end of round.
Round 8: *K2tog all round.
Break off yarn, thread through rem sts, pull up tightly and fasten off.
Felt the nest (see Introduction).
Pull into shape and place over an egg cup to dry.

Penguin Parade

This hilarious and fun-loving family of penguins is made up of characters each with their own distinct personality. Choose from a chef, clown, ballet dancer, horticultural expert or knitting fanatic.

MATERIALS

For Each Penguin

1 x 50 g (1¾ oz) ball black 4-ply (fingering/sports weight) knitting cotton

1 x 50 g (1¾ oz) ball white 4-ply (fingering/sports weight) knitting cotton

Oddment of pale yellow 4-ply (fingering/sports weight) yarn, for the beak and feet

2 x 4 mm (⅛ in) black beads, for the eyes

White stranded embroidery cotton

Polyester toy filling

Pair of 2 mm (UK 14/US 0) knitting needles

Pair of 2.75 mm (UK 12/US 2) knitting needles

Wool needle, for sewing up

Sewing needle

For Ballerina Penguin:

10 x 1 cm (³/₈ in) diameter pink flower beads

1 x 5 mm (¼ in) diameter pink button

20 x 5 cm (8 x 2 in) pink tulle or organza

Pink glass beads, for necklace

Polyester sewing cotton

6 mm (¼ in) pink crystal bead, for the headdress

3 mm (US 11) crochet hook

Beading needle

Pinking shears

Oddments of 4-ply (fingering/sports weight) yarn in pale and medium pink

For Knitting Nancy Penguin:

2 x 4 cm (1¼ in) wicker baskets, with a 1 cm (³/₈ in) diameter base

15 cm (6 in) of 1 cm (³/₈ in)-wide pink gingham ribbon

Straw hat, 7 cm (2¾ in) diameter

Oddments of 4-ply (fingering/sports weight) yarn in yellow, pink, orange, green, mauve, blue

2 cocktail sticks

2 round glass beads for the ends of the cocktail sticks, to make the knitting needles

Glue

Polyester thread

For Chef Penguin:

Oddment of red 4-ply (fingering/sports weight) yarn, for the scarf

Oddment of cream 4-ply (fingering/sports weight) yarn, for the apron and chef's hat

Wooden rolling pin and wooden bowl

For Gardening Penguin:

Small wooden bucket

Small wooden fork

Oddments of 4-ply (fingering/sports weight) yarn in grey, bright green, green bouclé, pale grey

3 x 5 mm (¼ in) diameter buttons, for the front of the waistcoat

For Clown Penguin:

1 x 1 cm (³/₈ in) diameter orange felt ball

Oddments of 4-ply (fingering/sports weight) yarn in blue, bright green, bright pink, orange, yellow, red, purple

Body and Head

Using 2.75 mm knitting needles and black yarn, cast on 6 sts.

Row 1: Purl.

Row 2: Inc in each st (12 sts).

Row 3: Purl.

Row 4: Inc in each sts (24 sts).

Row 5: Purl.

Row 6: *K1, inc in next st, rep from * to end (36 sts).

Row 7: Purl.

Row 8: *Inc in first st, K2, rep from * to end (48 sts).

Work another 19 rows st st, beg with a purl row.

Row 28: K10, Sl1, K1, psso, K2tog, K20, Sl1, K1, psso, K2tog, K10 (44 sts).

Row 29: Purl.

Row 30: K9, Sl1, K1, psso, K2tog, K18, Sl1, K1, psso, K2tog, K9 (40 sts).

Row 31: Purl.

Row 32: K8, Sl1, K1, psso, K2tog, K16, Sl1, K1, psso, K2tog, K8 (36 sts).

Row 33: Purl.

Row 34: *K2tog, K1, rep from * to end (24 sts).

Row 35: Purl.

Row 36: *K1, inc in next st, rep from * to end (36 sts).

Work 11 rows st st beg with a purl row.

Row 48: *K2tog, K1, rep from * to end (24 sts).

Row 49: Purl.

Row 50: K2tog all across.

Row 51: P2tog all across. Break off yarn. Thread through rem sts, pull up tightly and fasten off.

Tummy

Using 2.75 mm knitting needles and white cotton, cast on 8 sts at the base of the tummy.

Row 1: Purl.

Row 2: Inc in each st (16 sts).

Work 17 rows st st beg with a knit row.

Row 20: Sl1, K1, psso, K12, K2tog (14 sts).

Row 21: Purl.

Row 22: Sl1, K1, psso, K10, K2tog (12 sts).

Row 23: Purl.

Row 24: K2tog all across.

Cast off.

Wings

Make 2

Using 2.75 mm knitting needles and black, cast on 8 sts.

Row 1: Purl.

Row 1: Inc in each st (16 sts).

Work 13 rows st st beg with a purl row.

Row 16: *K2tog, K2 rep from * to end (12 sts).

Row 17: Purl.

Row 18: *K2tog, K1, rep from * to end (8 sts).

Row 19: Purl.

Row 20: K2tog all across.

Break off yarn, thread through rem sts, pull up tightly and fasten off. The cast-off end is the wing tip. With WS facing, sew the row ends tog using mattress st. (The pieces are too small to turn inside out).

Feet and Beak

Using 2.75 mm knitting needles and yellow, cast on 12 sts.

Row 1: Purl.

Row 2: Knit.

Row 3: Purl.

Row 4: K2tog all across. Break off yarn, thread through rem sts, pull up tightly and fasten off. Use a little polyester filling to stuff the beak and the feet and close the seam with small stitches. Ensure the feet are the same size. Set aside.

Take the penguin body piece and with RS tog, sew two-thirds of the back seam closed. Turn RS out. Stuff the penguin firmly. When you are happy with the shape of the body and the head, finish the back seam as invisibly as possible.

Pin the tummy on the front of the penguin. Ensure that you have stretched it out to make a rounded shape. Stitch all around, using white yarn and very small stitches.

Sew on the wings at the shoulder (neck level). Centre the beak on the face and stitch all around using very small stitches.

Place the feet tog at the front base of the body and stitch in place.

Put a pin where you want each eye to be or mark the position of each with a chalk pencil. Take three strands of white embroidery cotton and make a bullion loop knot with 20 wraps on the marked point. Do the same on the other side. Sew the black bead in the centre of the bullion loop knot.

Ballerina Penguin
Tutu Waistband

Using 2.75 mm knitting needles and pale pink yarn, cast on 70 sts. Work 2 rows garter st. Cast off.

Run a gathering stitch along one long edge of the organza or tulle. Cut the other long edge with pinking sheers so that it is just long enough to touch the ground when held from the penguin's waist. Gather the threads and attach the organza to the waistband and stitch in place. Sew the flower beads evenly around the waistband. Sew the tutu on the penguin.

Necklace

Slide half the pink glass beads on to a length of beading thread followed by the small pink button, then the rest of the glass beads. Dress on to the penguin, tie in a knot and hide the thread ends.

Headdress

Using crochet hook and dark pink, make 4 ch, join with a ss into a ring.

Round 1: (RS) 2 ch, 9dc in ring with dark pink, ss to top of 2 ch (10 sts).

Round 2: Using pale pink, 5 ch, 1 tr tr in each of next 9dc, ss to top of 5 ch. Fasten off.

Darn in end and form into a neat circle. Attach to the top and slightly to the side of the penguin's head. Sew one of the pale pink crystal beads into the centre of flower.

Knitting Nancy Penguin
Knitting Needles

Glue the glass beads to the end of the cocktail sticks. Using 2 mm knitting needles and blue 4-ply yarn, cast on 15 sts. Work in garter st for 4 cm (1¾ in). Transfer the knitting to the knitting needles you have made putting half the sts on one needle and the rest on the other needle. Darn in any loose yarn ends. Wrap the knitting around itself and pop into one of the baskets. Pop the basket over one of Nancy's wings and stitch in place.

Tie the pink gingham ribbon in a bow around the penguin's neck. Trim the ends if necessary.

Hat Decoration

Make 5 flowers (1 purple, 1 yellow, 1 pink, 1 orange, 1 blue) and 4 green leaves

Flowers

Using 2.75 mm knitting needles, and yarn, cast on 18 sts.

Row 1: Knit.

Row 2: P2tog all across.

Break off yarn, thread through rem sts, pull up tightly and fasten off.

Leaves

Using 2.75 mm knitting needles and green 4-ply, cast on 8 sts.

Row 1: K2, K4, winding yarn twice around needle on each st, K2.

Cast off, dropping the extra st on each of the centre 4 sts.

Darn in all ends. Stitch to hat.

Flowers for Basket

Make 2 pink, 1 orange, 1 yellow

Using 2.75 mm knitting needles and colour of choice, cast on 6 sts.

Row 1: Inc in every st.

Rows 2, 4, 6 and 8: Purl.

Row 3: Inc in every st (24 sts).

Row 5: K2tog all across.

Row 7: K2tog all across.

Row 9: K2tog all across.

Break off yarn, thread through rem sts, pull up tightly and fasten off.

Make up as for hat flowers.

Stems

Using 2.25 mm double-pointed knitting needles and green 4-ply, cast on 3 sts.

Make a 3 cm (1¼ in) I-cord. Fasten off.

Attach one end of the I-cord to the base of the flower and the other end to the base of the basket. Once all the flowers are in the basket, stitch the basket to the other wing.

Chef Penguin

Hat

Using 2.75 mm knitting needles and cream yarn, cast on 34 sts.

Work 4 rows st st, beg with a knit row.

Row 5: Purl.

Work 7 rows st st beg with a purl row.

Row 13: Inc in every st (68 sts).

Row 14: Purl.

Row 15: *K1, inc in next st, rep from * to end.

Work 3 rows st st beg with a purl row.

Row 19: *Sl1, K2tog, psso, rep from * to last st, K1 (35 sts).

Row 20: Purl.

Row 21: K2tog, all across to last st, K1.

Break off yarn, thread through rem sts, pull up tightly and fasten off.

With RS facing, sew back seam, turn up the hem to the inside at the purl row. Add a little polyester toy filling to puff up the top of the chef's hat and pop onto the head. Stitch all around, ensuring that the seam is at the back.

Apron

Using 2.75 mm knitting needles and cream yarn, cast on 16 sts.

Next row: Knit.

Next row: K1, purl to last st, K1.

Rep these two rows another 5 times.

Work 3 rows garter st.

Cast off.

Apron Ties

Using 2.75 mm knitting needles and cream yarn, cast on 74 sts. Work 3 rows garter st. Cast off.

Fold the apron ties in half and mark the centre. Position the main piece of the apron in the centre of the ties RS facing and stitch tog. Darn in any loose ends. Cross over the ties on the back of the penguin and stitch in place. If the apron has a tendency to curl up you may need to add a small stitch to the front to prevent this.

Necktie

Using 2.75 mm knitting needles and red yarn, cast on 72 sts. Work 2 rows garter st.

**Row 3: K7, turn, knit to end.

Row 4: K5, turn, knit to end.

Row 5: K3, turn, knit to end.

Knit all across ***

Rep from ** to *** once.

Cast off.

Darn in all ends.

Dress on to penguin. Cross over in the front, under the beak and hold in place with a stitch.

Stitch the rolling pin to one flipper and the wooden bowl to the other.

Gardening Penguin

Scarf

Using 2.75 mm knitting needles and bright green, cast on 90 sts.

Knit 1 row.

Cast off.

Darn in all ends. Knot around grandpa's neck.

Cap

Using 2.75 mm knitting needles and grey yarn, cast on 36 sts.

Work in K1, P1 rib for 2 rows.

Row 3: *Inc in first st, K1, rep from * to end of row (54 sts).

Rows 4, 6, 8, 10, 12 and 14: Purl.

Row 5: *K2, inc in next st, rep from * to end of row (72 sts).

Row 7: *K7, K2tog, rep from * to end.

Row 9: *K6, K2tog, rep from * to end.

Row 11: *K5, K2tog, rep from * to end.

Row 13: *K4, K2tog, rep from * to end.

Row 15: K2tog all across.

Purl 1 row.

Row 17: K2tog all across.

Break off yarn, thread through rem sts, pull up tightly and fasten off.

Peak

Using 2.75 mm knitting needles and grey yarn, cast on 12 sts.

Beg with a purl row, work 3 rows st st.

Row 4: K2tog, at beg and end of row.

Row 5: Purl.

Row 6: K2tog all across.

Row 7: Purl.

Row 8: Inc in every st.

Row 9: Inc in first st, purl to last st, inc in last st.

Work 6 rows st st beg with a knit row. Cast off.

Stitch centre back seam of main piece of cap. Fold peak in half, WS tog, stitch to underside of hat with the peak facing out.

Bobble

Using 2.25 mm double-pointed knitting needles and light grey 4-ply yarn, cast on 1 st.

Inc into front, back, front, back, front of this st (5 sts).

Row 2: Knit.

Row 3: Purl.

Row 4: Knit.

Row 5: Purl

Row 6: Knit, don't turn, slip *second st over the first st, repeat from * until 1 st rem on needle, fasten off. Run a gathering thread around the outside edge of the bobble and draw up to form a tight ball. Attach to the top of the cap.

Waistcoat

Back

Using 2.75 mm knitting needles and green bouclé, cast on 42 sts.

Work in garter st for 2.5 cm (1 in).

Cast off 8 sts at beg of next 2 rows (26 sts).

Work another 2 cm (¾ in) garter st.

Cast on 8 sts at beg of next 2 rows

Knit 1 row.

Cast off.

Fronts

Make 2

Using 2.75 mm knitting needles and green boucle 4-ply, cast on 5 sts.

Knit 1 row.

Row 2: Inc 1 st at beg of next row. K to end

Row 3: Inc 1 st at end of next row. K to end

Rep these 2 rows until there are 18 sts.

Knit 1 row without shaping.

Row 23: Cast off 6 sts at straight edge.

Cont in garter st without further shaping until front edge measures 1.5 cm (5/8 in).

**Next row: Knit to last 2 sts, K2tog (front edge).

***Next row: Knit.

Rep these 2 rows once.

Knit 2 rows.

Rep from ** to *** 3 times.

Cast off.

Sew shoulder seams of fronts and back tog. Sew sides of fronts and backs together. Pop on to the penguin and stitch in place. Sew three tiny buttons down one front.

Attach the wooden bucket to one wing, and the wooden fork to the other.

Clown Penguin

Collar Frill

Using 2.75 mm knitting needles and green, cast on 10 sts.

Knit 2 rows garter st.

Row 3: **Cast off 7 sts, knit to end, turn, K3, join in blue, cast on 7 sts

Knit 2 rows.

Rep from ** using the following colour scheme: pink, orange, yellow, red, purple, green.

Complete 3 repeats of the colourscheme and then cast off.

Darn in all ends. Wrap the collar frill around the penguin's neck and stitch in place.

Hat

Using 2.75 mm knitting needles and green, cast on 36 sts.

Work 4 rows st st beg with a knit row.

Row 5: Purl

Beg with a purl row, work another 3 rows green and then 2 rows blue st st.

Work stripe patt as folls and AT THE SAME TIME keep decreases correct: 2 rows each pink, orange, yellow, red, purple, green, blue, pink.

Dec row: K2tog, K14, K2togtbl, K2tog, K14, K2togtbl.

Next and alt rows: Purl.

Dec row: K2tog, K12, K2togtbl, K2tog, K12, K2togtbl.

Dec row: K2tog, K10, K2togtbl, K2tog, K10, K2togtbl.

Dec row: K2tog, K8, K2togtbl, K2tog, K8, K2togtbl.

Cont decreasing in this manner on alt rows until 6 sts rem. Break off yarn, thread through rem sts, pull up tightly and fasten off.

   With RS tog, stitch back seam. Darn in all ends and turn up hem to the inside. Attach the orange felt ball to the top. Stitch the penguin's hat to the top of his head using very small stitches.

Pom Poms

Make 4 (1 each of orange, pink, green and blue)

Using 2.25 mm double-pointed knitting needles and yarn, cast on 1 st.

Inc into front, back, front, back, front of this st (5 sts).

Row 2: Knit.

Row 3: Purl.

Row 4: Knit.

Row 5: Purl.

Row 6: Knit, don't turn. *Slip second st over the first st, repeat from * until 1 st rem on needle, fasten off.

Run a gathering thread around the outside edge of the bobble and draw up to form a tight ball. Stitch the pom poms evenly to the penguin's tummy.

Patchwork Turtle

Percy is a lovely colourful turtle made up of hexagonal shapes which have been knitted on three double-pointed knitting needles and then filled with polyester toy filling. These are then sewn together to create the shell. The legs, head, tail and underbody are worked separately and then sewn in place. A little flower adorns the head.

MATERIALS

Small amounts (less than 25 g/1 oz of each colour) 4-ply (fingering/sports weight) yarn in bright blue, royal blue, yellow, orange, red, bright green and bright pink

Set of 2.25 mm ((UK 13/US 1) double-pointed knitting needles

Pair of 2 mm ((UK 14/US 0) double-pointed knitting needles

Wool needle, for sewing up

Polyester toy filling

Black stranded embroidery cotton

3 mm (UK 11) crochet hook

Hexagons

Make 7

Using 2 x 2.25 mm double-pointed knitting needles and your choice of yarn colour, cast on 20 sts.

Have the needle with the stitches on in your left hand and two empty needles in your right hand. *Slip the first st purlwise onto the needle closest to you, now slip the next st on to the back needle, rep from * until all sts are on 2 needles. You will have 10 on each. Knitting is worked backward and forward in rows with increases at the sides. Use the third needle to knit with.

Row 1: Inc in first st, knit to last 2 sts, inc in next sts, K1. Turn work and repeat with sts on the other needle.

Row 2: Knit.

Repeat rows 1 and 2 until you have 40 sts, 20 on each needle.

Dec row: Sl1, K1, psso, K to last 2 sts, K2tog. Repeat with sts on other needle.

Next row: Knit.

Repeat these 2 rows until there are 10 sts left on each needle.

At this point, fill the hexagon with polyester toy filling. Do not overfill. Either graft stitches tog or cast off.

Shell

Place one shape in the centre and the other six hexagons around. Stitch the side seams so the central hexagon is enclosed and the other hexagons form a ring around it. Set aside.

Underbody

Using crochet hook and bright blue, make a slip knot and then 6 ch. Form into a ring.

Round 1: Work 12dc into ring, join with a ss.

Round 2: 1 ch, *2dc into each dc, join with a ss.

Round 3: 1 ch, *1dc, 2dc into next dc rep from * to end of round, join with a ss.

Round 4: 1 ch, *2dc, 2dc into next dc rep from * to end of round, join with a ss.

Round 5: 1 ch, *3dc, 2dc into next dc rep from * to end of round, join with a ss.

Round 6: 1 ch, *4dc, 2dc into next dc rep from * to end of round, join with a ss.

Round 7: 1 ch, 1dc into every dc to end of round, join with a ss. Fasten off.

Stuff underbody firmly to make a curved shape and stitch below the patchwork shell.

Feet

Make 4

Using 2 mm knitting needles and, bright blue 4-ply, cast on 15 sts.

Beg with a knit row, work 5 rows st st.

Row 6: P1, P2tog all across.

Break off yarn, thread through rem sts, pull up tightly and fasten off.

Place WS tog and sew the side seam. Stuff the legs firmly leaving the tops open. When all four are complete, pin them in position, evenly spaced, on the underside of the body and when you are happy with the position, stitch in place using very small stitches so the turtle doesn't wobble.

Tail

Using 2 mm knitting keedles and bright green yarn, cast on 5 sts.

Row 1: Knit.

Row 2: Inc in first st, purl to last st, inc in last st.

Row 3: Knit.

Rep these 2 rows twice more (11 sts).

Work another 2 rows st st.

Next row: P1, (P2tog five times).

Break off yarn, thread through rem sts, pull up tightly and fasten off.

With WS tog, sew the side seam. The gathered end will be attached to the turtle.

Head

Using set of double-pointed knitting needles and bright green, cast on 18 sts, (6, 6, 6). Join into a ring, being careful not to twist the sts.

Knit 4 rounds

Round 5: Inc in first st, K5, M1 in next st, K12 (20 sts). Work another 3 rounds st st.

Round 9: Sl1, K1, psso, K4, K2tog, K4, K2tog, K6 (17 sts).

Round 10: Knit.

Round 11: Sl1, K1, psso, K2, K2tog, K5, K2tog, K4 (14 sts).

Round 12: Knit.

Round 13: Sl1, K1, psso, K1, K2tog, K3, K2tog, K5 (11 sts).

Round 14: Knit

Round 15: K6, K2tog, K3 (10 sts).

Round 16: K2tog 5 times.

Break off yarn, thread through rem sts, pull up tightly and fasten off.

Stitch the seam and then fill the head with polyester toy filling.

Stitch in place closing the opening as you attach the head to the underside of the turtle.

Face

Use a chalk pencil to mark the position of the eyes. Using three strands of black embroidery cotton and an embroidery needle, work French knots for the eyes. Work the mouth in stem stitch.

Flower

Using crochet hook and blue, make a slip knot. Make 4 ch, join into a ring.

Round 1: 1 ch, work 8dc into ring. Ss into first ch.

Round 2: *3 ch miss 1dc, ss into next dc, rep from * right around the ring ending with ss into first of the 3 ch. Fasten off. Darn in all ends.

Attach flower to the top of head.

Mousey Mouse

With his softly felted coat this little mouse is a very tactile toy that will fit comfortably in any pocket. You could add a squeak when you are stuffing the insides, just make sure that it is securely wrapped in toy filling and the seams are sturdy.

MATERIALS

Oddment of grey 4-ply (fingering/sports weight) yarn, for the mouse

Oddment of red 4-ply (fingering/sports weight) yarn, for the stocking

Oddment of white eyelash yarn, for the top of the stocking

Pair of 2 mm (UK14/US 0) knitting needles

Set of 2.25 mm (UK 13/US 1) double-pointed knitting needles

Wool needle, for sewing up

Black stranded embroidery cotton

White stranded embroidery cotton

10 cm (4 in) x 5 mm (¼ in) wide red ribbon, for hanging loop

Polyester toy filling

Red polyester sewing cotton

Body

Using 2 mm knitting needles and grey, cast on 7 sts.
Begin with a knit row, work 2 rows st st.

Row 3: K2, inc into next 2 sts, K3.

Next and alt rows: Purl.

Row 5: K3, inc into next 2 sts, K4.

Row 7: K4, inc into next 2 sts, K5.

Cont increasing in the centre 2 sts in this manner until there are 31 sts.

Work 3 rows st st without further shaping.

Next row: K1, (Sl1, K1, psso) 7 times, K1, (K2tog 7 times), K1.

Next row: K1, (Sl1, K1, psso) 3 times, K3, (K2tog 3 times), K1 (11 sts).

Purl 1 row.

Break off yarn, thread through rem sts, pull up tightly and fasten off.

Ears

Make 2

Using 2 mm knitting needles and yarn, cast on 3 sts.

Row 1: Inc in first st, K2.

Row 2: Inc in first st, P to end.

Row 3: Inc in first st, K to end.

Row 4: Inc in first st, P to end.

Row 5: Knit.

Break off yarn, thread through rem sts, pull up tightly and fasten off. This is the base of the ear.

With RS tog, stitch underneath seam part closed. Turn the mouse right side out and begin stuffing firmly. Cont to fill and sew the remainder of the seam closed.

Position the ears on each side of the head and pin in place. Stitch firmly in position.

Tail

Using 2 x 2.25 mm double-pointed knitting needles and yarn make a 2-stitch I-cord, 9–10 cm (4 in) long. Fasten off. Attach securely to the mouse's bottom.

Nose and Eyes

Using two strands of black embroidery cotton, make a French Knot for each eye. Make a French knot in white for the nose. Add some whiskers if you like.

The Tiniest Pig of All

This is the smallest toy in the collection and quite cute too. Don't be daunted by his small proportions as he is easily knitted on two needles.

MATERIALS

Oddment of pale pink 4-ply (fingering/sports weight) yarn, for the pig
Oddment of bright green 4-ply (fingering/sports weight) yarn, for the scarf
Pair of 2 mm (UK 14/US 0) knitting needles
Pair of 2.25 mm (UK 13/US 1) knitting needles
Wool needle, for sewing up
Black stranded embroidery cotton
Sewing needle
Polyester toy filling

MEASUREMENTS

4 x 6 cm (1¾ x 2¼ in)

Body

Using 2 mm knitting needles and pink, cast on 7 sts.
Row 1: Knit.
Row 2: Purl, inc 1 st in first and last st (9 sts).
Row 3: Inc in every st (18 sts).
Row 4: Purl.
Row 5: *Inc, K1, rep from * to end (27 sts).
Row 6: Purl.
Row 7: Knit.
Row 8: Purl.
Row 9: *K1, inc in next st, K1, rep from * to end (36 sts).
Work another 7 rows st st without shaping.
Row 17: *K1, K2tog, K1, rep from * to end (27 sts).
Row 18: Purl.
Row 19: Knit.
Row 20: Knit.
Row 21: *K1, K2tog, rep from * to end (18 sts).
Row 22: Purl
Row 23: K2tog all across.
Break off yarn, thread through rem sts, pull up tightly and fasten off.
With RS together stitch two-thirds of the tummy seam. Turn RS out and firmly stuff the body. Close the remainder of the seam. Run a gathering thread around the cast-on sts, pull up tightly and fasten off.

Head

Using 2 mm knitting needles and pink, cast on 16 sts.
Row 1: K3, (inc in next st twice), K5, (inc in next st twice), K4 (20 sts).
Row 2: Purl.
Row 3: K4, (inc in next st twice), K7, (inc in next st twice), K5 (24 sts).
Work another 5 rows st st without shaping.
Row 9: *K1, K2tog, K1, rep from * to end (18 sts).
Row 10: Purl.

Row 11: Knit.
Row 12: Purl.
Row 13: *K1, K2tog, rep from * to end.
Break off yarn, thread through rem sts, pull up tightly and fasten off.
Stitch head seam from gathered top edge to the lower edge. Use very small pieces of polyester toy filling to stuff the head firmly. The head seam will be under the chin.

Ears

Make 2
Using 2 mm knitting needles and pink, cast on 5 sts
Work 2 rows st st.
Row 3: Sl1, K1, psso, K to last 2 sts, K2tog.
Row 4: Purl.
Row 5: Sl1, K1, psso, K2tog.
Row 6: Purl
Row 7: K2tog. Fasten off.
Stitch the ears to the top of the pig's head ensuring that they are evenly placed. The points will roll upward.

Face

Using 2 strands of black embroidery cotton, work two French knots for eyes just above the snout and a few mm ($1/8$ in) apart. Make two tiny straight stitches for nostrils on the end of the snout.

Tail

Take two lengths of pink yarn and make a twisted cord. Knot off a 2 cm (¾ in) length and stitch to the pig's bottom.

Snout

Using 2 x 2 mm double-pointed knitting needles and pink 4 ply, cast on 1 st.
K, P, K, P, K into same st (5 sts).
Row 1: Knit.
Row 2: Purl.
Row 3: Knit.
Row 4: Purl.
Row 5: Knit, do not turn, * slip second stitch on right-hand needle over first, rep from * until 1 st remains.
Fasten off.
Run a gathering thread around the bobble and draw up to make a neat round shape. Darn in any loose ends and stitch to the centre of the pig's nose.

Legs

Make 4
Using 2 mm knitting needles and pink, cast on 6 sts.
Work 4 rows st st, beg with a knit row.
Break off yarn, thread through rem sts, pull up tightly and fasten off.
Roll up the leg very tightly and stitch down the long seam. Stitch the end closed. Pin the legs evenly to the underside of the pig so that it will stand.

Scarf

Using 2.25 mm knitting needles and bright green, cast on 35 sts. Work 2 rows garter st. Cast off.
Darn in ends. Knot around the neck.

Twisted Cords

Cut a length of yarn four times longer than the desired length of the twisted cord. Fold the strand in half and make a slip knot at the cut ends. Pass the slip knot over a doorknob, hold the other end and stand far enough away so that the yarn hangs in mid-air and does not touch the ground.

Slip a crochet hook into the loop in your hand and, while still holding the yarn in the left hand, twirl the hook to twist the yarn around itself. Continue twisting until the yarn is quite taut and evenly twisted.

Still holding one end of the yarn in your left hand, with your right hand pinch the twisted strand midway between yourself and the doorknob. Bring the ends of the yarn together by moving toward the doorknob, but DO NOT LET GO OF THE MIDDLE OF THE TWISTED YARN. You will notice as you let go of the pinched midpoint of the twisted yarn it will twist around itself forming a plied cord.

Still holding tight to the ends so the twisted cord doesn't unwind itself, loose the yarn end from the doorknob and tie both ends together. You can run your finger between the cords to even out the twists, if necessary.

Oliver the Christmas Owl

Related to the Owl Family, Oliver the Christmas Owl is distinguished by his snowy white tummy, yellow beak, seasonal hat and smart bow tie. He's all ready to celebrate the festive season in style.

MATERIALS

Small amount (less than 25 g/1 oz of dark grey 4-ply (fingering/sports weight) yarn

Oddment of yellow 4-ply (fingering/sports weight) yarn, for the feet and beak

Oddment of red 4-ply (fingering/sports weight) yarn, for the hat and bow tie

Oddment of white angora, for the tummy and hat brim

10 cm (4 in) square of white felt, for the eyes

Black stranded embroidery cotton, for the features

Air-soluble marker pen

Embroidery needle

Pair of 2 mm (UK14/US 0) knitting needles

Wool needle, for sewing up

Polyester fibre filling

Note

Owl is worked on 2 needles and has a centre back seam. Careful sewing will make this invisible.

Body

Using dark grey yarn, cast on 7 sts.

Row 1: *K1, yfwd, rep from * to end (13 sts).

Row 2: Purl.

Row 3: K1, *yfwd, K2, rep from * to end (19 sts).

Row 4: Purl.

Rep last 2 rows once (28 st).

Row 7: K3, *yfwd, K3, rep from * to last 4 sts, K4 (36 sts).

Row 8: Purl.

Row 9: K2, *yfwd, K4, rep from * to last 2 sts, K2 (44 sts).

Row 10: *K1, P1, rep from * to end.

Row 11: *P1, K1, rep from * to end

Work another 11 rows moss st.

Row 23: Moss st 16 sts as set in dark grey, join in white angora yarn for tummy panel and K14 sts, carrying grey yarn across the back of work, moss st 16 sts dark grey.

Row 24: Moss st 16 st dark grey, purl 14 sts white, moss st 16 sts grey.

Repeat these 2 rows another 8 times each.

Row 41: Moss st 17 sts dark grey, K12 white, moss st 17 sts dark grey.

Row 42: Moss st 18 sts dark grey, P10 white, moss st 18 sts dark grey.

Row 43: Moss st 19 sts dark grey, K8 white, moss st 19 sts dark grey.

Row 44: Moss st 20 sts dark grey, P6 white, moss st 20 sts dark grey. Break off white yarn and continue in grey only.

Work another 8 rows moss st.

Dec row: K2, *K2tog, K2, rep from * to last st, K1.

Next row: Purl.

Rep last 2 rows once.

Next row: K2, *K2tog, K1, rep from * to last st, K1.

Next row: Purl.

Repeat last 2 rows once.

Next row: K2tog all across.

Break off yarn. Thread through rem sts, pull up tightly and fasten off.

Wings

Make 2

Using dark grey, cast on 11 sts.

Work 2 rows moss st.

Next row: P2tog, moss st to end.

Rep this row until 1 sts rem.

Fasten off.

Feet

Using yellow yarn, cast on 20 sts.

Row 1: Knit.

**Dec 1 st at each end of every row until 12 sts rem.

Next row: Knit.

Inc 1 st at each end of every row until there are 20 sts.

Next row: Knit***

Rep from ** to *** once.

Fold foot section in half and stitch all around. Sew to underside of owl with the shaped toe section facing forward.

Beak

Using yellow yarn, cast on 1 st.

Row 1: Inc in back and front of stitch (3 sts).

Row 2: Purl.

Row 3: Inc in first and last st (5 sts).

Row 4: Purl.

Row 5: Inc in first and last st (7 sts).

Row 6: Purl.

Cast off

Fold beak tog WS facing. Stitch edges together and then sew on to the owl between the eyes with the point facing down toward the toes.

With RS tog, stitch the centre back seam closed for two-thirds of the way. Turn RS out. Stuff very firmly with small pieces of polyester fibre filling to make a cylindrical shape. Stitch seam closed gathering the cast-on edge shut as you sew.

Eyes

Cut 2 felt circles 1.5 cm (^{5}/$_8$ in) diameter. Draw a semi-circular eyelid on each using an air-soluble marker, then stem stitch over the drawn lines with black embroidery cotton. Sew the eyes on the owl. If you want your owl to be awake you could sew on some tiny black buttons instead.

Hat

Using white angora, cast on 48 sts.
Work 4 rows of st st. Break off white and join in red.
Work another 4 rows st st.
Row 9: *K4, K2tog, rep from * to end.
Work 3 rows st st.
Row 13: *K3, K2tog, rep from * to end.
Work 3 rows st st.
Row 17: *K2, K2tog, rep from * to end.
Work 3 rows st st.
Row 21: *K1, K2tog, rep from * to end.
Work 3 rows st st.
Row 25: *K2tog, rep from * to end.
Work 3 rows st st.
Row 29: *K2tog, rep from * to end.
Break off yarn, thread through rem sts, pull up tightly and fasten off.
With RS tog, sew centre back seam and darn in any loose ends. Stitch to the top of the head.

Bow Tie

Using red yarn, cast on 18 sts
Work 20 rows st st.
Cast off.
Fold in half, WS facing and sew the short edges tog. Turn RS out. Wrap a length of red yarn tightly around the centre of the piece to form the wings of the bow tie. Stitch through the centre to secure. Stitch in place.

Index